Oprah Winfrey

MEDIA LEGEND AND INSPIRATION TO MILLIONS

By Diane Dakers

Crabtree Publishing Company
www.crabtreebooks.com

Crabtree Publishing Company
www.crabtreebooks.com

Author: Diane Dakers
Publishing plan research and development: Reagan Miller
Project coordinator: Mark Sachner, Water Buffalo Books
Editors: Mark Sachner, Lynn Peppas
Proofreader: Wendy Scavuzzo
Indexer: Gini Holland
Editorial director: Kathy Middleton
Photo researcher: Water Buffalo Books
Designer: Westgraphix/Tammy West
Production coordinator and prepress technician: Margaret Amy Salter
Print coordinator: Margaret Amy Salter

Written, developed, and produced by Water Buffalo Books

Publisher's note:
All quotations in this book come from original sources and contain the spelling and grammatical inconsistencies of the original text. Some of the quotations may also contain terms that are no longer in use and may be considered inappropriate or offensive. The use of such terms is for the sake of preserving the historical and literary accuracy of the sources and should not be seen as encouraging or endorsing the use of such terms today.

Photographs and reproductions:
Alamy: © WENN Ltd: pp. 6 (second from top), 9 (top); © Witold Skrypczak: p. 20; © Globe Photos/ZUMAPRESS.com: pp. 61, 72; Moviestore collection Ltd: p. 65 (top); © United Archives GmbH: p. 67; Photo by Paul Fenton/ ZUMA KPA: p. 77; © Gallo Images: p. 84. **Corbis:** © Francis Dean: p. 12 (top); © Walter McBride/Retna Ltd.: pp. 28; 38; © Reuters: p. 43; © Bettmann: p. 49; © Najlah Feanny/CORBIS SABA: p. 50; © AP: p. 56; © Neal Preston: p. 58; © Douglas Kirkland: p. 65 (bottom); © Nancy Kaszerman/ZUMA: p. 71; © Michael Lewis: p. 78; © Louise Gubb: p. 82; © Jason Braverman/ZUMA Press: p. 95. **Getty Images:** David Livingston: cover (left); Michelly Rall: cover (right); Jeff Vespa: p. 6 (top); RJ Sangosti: p. 32; Afro Newspaper/Gado: p. 45; Robin Platzer: p. 47; Taro Yamasaki: p. 57; MANDEL NGAN/AFP/ Getty Images: p. 89; Handout: p. 90; AFP/Stringer: p. 92; The Washington Post: p. 93; Boston Globe: p. 102; Thomas Cooper: p. 103 (top); Bloomberg: p. 103 (bottom). **Gini Holland:** p. 27 (top). **Public domain:** pp. 7, 11 (bottom right), 12 (bottom), 14, 17, 18, 29, 35, 39, 40, 68. **Mark Sachner:** pp. 26, 27 (bottom). **Shutterstock:** Jaguar PS: p. 1; Ron Foster Sharif: p. 4 (top); Everett Collection: pp. 5, 6 (bottom, second from bottom), 17, 31, 42, 49, 71, 85, 89; Featureflash: pp. 9 (bottom), 54, 64; Henryk Sadura: p. 22; KennStilger47: p. 23; s_bukley: p. 96; Rena Schild: p. 98; Debby Wong: p. 99. **Superstock:** PARAMOUNT PICTURES/Album: p. 83; FOLLOW THROUGH PROD/ SALAMANDER PIC/LAURA ZISKIN PR/Album: p. 97. **Wikipedia/Creative Commons:** pp. 4 (bottom), 10 (top left, right), 11 (top left, middle left, bottom left, top right, middle right), 52, 60, 100; Parkwood: p. 10 (lower left); Raymond Boyd: p. 15; photo by Alan Light: p. 75.

Cover: Foreground: While aboard the International Space Station (ISS) between December 2012 and May 2013, astronaut Chris Hadfield became the first Canadian to lead an ISS mission. Background: He also built up a powerful social media presence, tweeting, telling stories, singing songs, and beaming back to Earth thousands of photos with captivating descriptions. Here, Chris is shown on a large screen, playing his guitar and singing with school kids via a video link.

Library and Archives Canada Cataloguing in Publication

Dakers, Diane, author
Oprah Winfrey : media legend and inspiration to millions / Diane Dakers.

(Crabtree groundbreaker biographies)
Includes index.
Issued in print and electronic formats.
ISBN 978-0-7787-2559-6 (bound).--ISBN 978-0-7787-2561-9 (paperback).--ISBN 978-1-4271-9991-1 (pdf).--ISBN 978-1-4271-9989-8 (html)

1. Winfrey, Oprah--Juvenile literature. 2. Women television personalities--United States--Biography--Juvenile literature. 3. African American television personalities--United States--Biography--Juvenile literature. 4. Motion picture actors and actresses--United States--Biography--Juvenile literature. 5. African American motion picture actors and actresses--United States--Biography--Juvenile literature. I. Title. II. Series: Crabtree groundbreaker biographies

PN1992.4.W56D35 2015 j791.45092 C2015-903385-3
C2015-903386-1

Library of Congress Cataloging-in-Publication Data

Dakers, Diane.
Oprah winfrey : media legend and inspiration to millions / Diane Dakers.
pages cm. -- (Crabtree groundbreaker biographies)
Includes index.
ISBN 978-0-7787-2559-6 (reinforced library binding) -- ISBN 978-0-7787-2561-9 (pbk.) -- ISBN 978-1-4271-9991-1 (electronic pdf) -- ISBN 978-1-4271-9989-8 (electronic html)
1. Winfrey, Oprah--Juvenile literature. 2. Television personalities--Biography--Juvenile literature. 3. African American television personalities--Biography--Juvenile literature. 4. Actors--United States--Biography--Juvenile literature. 5. African American actors--Biography--Juvenile literature. I. Title.
PN1992.4.W56D35 2016
791.4502'8092--dc23
[B]

2015022179

Crabtree Publishing Company
www.crabtreebooks.com 1-800-387-7650 Printed in Canada/102015/IH20150821

In Canada: We acknowledge the financial support of the Government of Canada through the Canada Book Fund for our publishing activities.

Published in Canada
Crabtree Publishing
616 Welland Ave.
St. Catharines, Ontario
L2M 5V6

Published in the United States
Crabtree Publishing
PMB 59051
350 Fifth Ave., 59th Floor
New York, NY 10118

Published in the United Kingdom
Crabtree Publishing
Maritime House
Basin Road North, Hove
BN41 1WR

Published in Australia
Crabtree Publishing
3 Charles Street
Coburg North
VIC, 3058

Contents

Above: Oprah Winfrey shares a warm moment with David Letterman as he interviews her as part of a lecture series in Muncie, Indiana. By the time they retired from their talk shows—Oprah in 2011, after 25 years, and Dave in 2015, after 33 years—they had become icons in their respective fields of daytime and late-night TV. Although neither Oprah nor Dave seemed 100 percent clear on either the cause or even the existence of a supposedly 20-year feud, they had already famously "made up" by the time they appeared here, in 2012.

Above right: Oprah is shown in Copenhagen, Denmark, in 2009, during a campaign to support Chicago's bid for the 2016 Summer Olympic Games. Despite efforts by Oprah and other high-profile personalities with Chicago ties, including Michael Jordan and Barack and Michelle Obama, Chicago lost out to Rio de Janeiro, Brazil.

Chapter 1
Talking the Talk

Oprah gives her friend Elmo a kiss during a 2004 benefit in New York City on behalf of the Sesame Workshop, which is behind the production of Sesame Street *and other children's programming.*

In 1976, when she was just 22 years old, Oprah Winfrey hit the big time—or so she thought. She had just landed a job as co-anchor of the evening newscast at a television station in Baltimore, Maryland. Although she was young and inexperienced, Oprah had a rich voice and a wonderful on-air presence. She was also a natural storyteller. She beat out more than 100 other hopefuls for the plum position. "I came in naive, unskilled, not really knowing anything about the business—or about life," said Oprah almost 40 years later. Still, WJZ-TV took a chance on her.

Change of Plans

Oprah was thrilled with her new, high-profile position—but it turned out that the TV station wasn't so thrilled with Oprah. She simply didn't have what it took to do the job properly. After just eight months, station management removed her from the anchor desk. It was a public humiliation, and Oprah was "devastated."

Because she was under contract, though, WJZ couldn't fire her. Instead, they gave Oprah a shot at co-hosting a new morning talk show. At first, she didn't want to do it. She thought that she wouldn't be taken seriously if she worked on a talk show.

George Clooney

Tom Hanks

Mariah Carey

Denzel Washington

Oprah with a few of her celebrity friends and interview guests.

Oprah cried and begged her boss *not* to put her on the talk show—but he insisted she try it.

In 1978, Oprah reluctantly began co-hosting *People are Talking*. It wasn't at all what she had expected. Instantly, she knew that this was where she belonged, that "[she] had found a home for [her]self."

As quickly as Oprah realized she had found her home, so did her audiences. They loved the warm, natural, curious young woman with the gift of good conversation. Within a month, *People are Talking* was the top-rated program in its time slot. It even beat out talk show host Phil Donahue, who was then known as "the king of talk."

Six years later, when a major Chicago television station was looking for a new host for its morning talk show, Oprah auditioned and got the job. At age 30, Oprah moved to Illinois and became the new host of *A.M. Chicago*.

Oprah was such a hit with her audiences that *A.M. Chicago* was renamed *The Oprah Winfrey Show* a year after she got there. A year after that, *The Oprah Winfrey Show* went national. Soon to become popularly known simply as *Oprah*, the program would stay on the air for 25 years.

During the lifetime of *The Oprah Winfrey Show*, Oprah interviewed countless celebrities, such as Michael Jackson, George Clooney, Julia Roberts, Denzel Washington, Tom Hanks, Tom Cruise, John Travolta, and Mariah Carey. Talk show host Ellen DeGeneres "came out" as a lesbian on Oprah's show in 1997. Canadian superstar singer Celine Dion appeared on the program 28 times—more often than anyone else.

Talking on TV

As soon as television began beaming into living rooms across the United States, talk shows were on the viewing schedule. The first TV talk show started in 1951 on Baltimore's WJZ-TV, the station where Oprah later launched her career. *The Tonight Show*, which started in 1954 and remains on-air today, is the world's longest-running late-night talk show.

Like most late-night talk shows to this day, early talk shows, regardless of what time of day they were on, featured a host interviewing guests. In 1967, Phil Donahue created the first talk show in which the host also interacted with audiences. He also introduced shows that addressed social issues, rather than simply focusing on the careers of celebrity guests. For all he did in revolutionizing the format and focus of TV talk shows, Phil is considered the founder of the modern talk show and has often been called "the king of talk." *The Phil Donahue Show* (also known as *Donahue*), which ended in 1996, remains the longest-running daytime talk show in history. Many shows, including *The Oprah Winfrey Show*, followed in Phil's footsteps.

Two talk show legends, Johnny Carson (left) and Phil Donahue, on the set of The Phil Donahue Show *in 1970. Phil was the longest-serving host on daytime TV, with a run of 29 years (1967–1996), while Johnny had the longest run on late-night, hosting* The Tonight Show with Johnny Carson *for 30 years (1962–1992).*

Sometimes, Oprah's shows were scandalous, gossipy, and thought provoking—particularly in her early years—when she hosted racists, criminals, and other unpleasant characters. Other times, she provided viewers with information on a host of subjects and concerns. For example, she featured psychologists, doctors, and authors. Very often, Oprah's topics of discussion were uplifting, positive, and spiritual. She also featured makeovers, reunions, gift giveaways, and interviews with inspiring children.

Oprah had a knack for making each of her guests feel special. She gave them the courage to talk about their feelings, problems, successes, and failures. She was the friend who let them know their problems didn't make them weird or unlikable—because everyone has problems. Oprah encouraged her viewers to follow their dreams, to be the best they could be, and to be true to themselves. Said one media commentator:

"She really tapped into a deeply American idea of self-transformation and the power of the mind, that if we have the right attitude and positive thinking, we can transform our situation. Her message resonated because it tapped into these powerful economic, political, spiritual and social currents happening inside culture at the same time."

By the time *The Oprah Winfrey Show* aired for the last time, in May 2011, its host was one of the most powerful—and wealthiest—women in the world.

Oprah with friends and frequent interview guests Tom Cruise, shown right at a special tribute to Oprah in 2010, and Julia Roberts, shown below at the 2004 Academy Awards in Hollywood.

"[Oprah] is your down-to-Earth friend whose pals are Julia Roberts and Tom Cruise. She's the spiritual leader who is a workaholic and does an episode every year about all the expensive stuff she loves. She's a spiritual leader who doesn't choose a particular church. She's a woman who stands up for motherhood and family values but doesn't have kids. [Her fans] appreciate the fact they can turn on Oprah and see someone who seems like their best friend but gives them access to this amazing world."

TV critic Eric Deggans, 2011

First-Name Basis

Although Oprah Winfrey officially uses her first and last names, she is so well known around the world that most people identify her by her first name only. There are others, like Oprah, who are so famous they only need one name. In Oprah's case, it helps that her name is unusual, as are most other single-name celebrity names. Some, like Oprah, are real names. Others, like Eminem, are completely made up. (His real name is Marshall Bruce Mathers III; "Eminem" is a spelled-out version of the initials of his first and last names.) How many single-name celebs can you think of? Here are a few to start you off, along with their full names.

Adele
(Adele Laurie Blue Adkins)

Beyoncé
(Beyoncé Giselle Knowles)

Usher
(Usher Terry Raymond IV)

Shakira
(Shakira Isabel Mebarak Ripoll)

Sting
(Gordon Matthew Thomas Sumner)

Pink
(Alecia Beth Moore)

Bono
(Paul David Hewson)

Pharrell
(Pharrell Williams)

Madonna
(Madonna Louise Ciccone)

Cher
(Cherilyn Sarkisian)

"I want to be lean and clean for the future."
—Oprah's Aha Moment
THE OPRAH MAGAZINE
"Life is a big ol' canvas. And you have every combination of colors to paint with."
—Oprah
The MAKE-YOUR-DREAMS-REAL
Our Biggest, Best Summer Reading List Ever!
26 BOOKS YOU'LL LOVE
WIN A FANTASY GETAWAY
DR. OZ TO THE RESCUE
5 ACHES & PAINS YOU SHOULD NEVER IGNORE
HOW TO MAKE A VISION BOARD THAT REALLY WORKS
THE OPRAH MAGAZINE
DO WHAT YOU LOVE!
Find it
Go for it
Live creatively
ever after
SHOPPING HANDBO
"Say Yes to Life!"
—OPRAH
28 Genius Ways to Get Unstuck and
OWN
OPRAH WINFREY NETWORK

More Than Just a Talk Show Host

Soon after *The Oprah Winfrey Show* first took to the airwaves, Oprah founded her own production company. Called Harpo Studios ("Harpo" is "Oprah" spelled backward), the company produced Oprah's talk show, along with many other TV programs and feature films. In 2000, Oprah launched a magazine called *O, The Oprah Magazine.* A few years later, she established Oprah Radio and a cable TV network called OWN, which stands for the Oprah Winfrey Network.

Thanks to all these business interests, in 2003, Oprah became the first female African-American billionaire in U.S. history. She is only the second African-American billionaire ever, after media executive Bob Johnson, who first made the list in 2001. Since 2009, Oprah has been the only African American in the billionaire's club.

As wealthy as she is, Oprah has always been generous with her money. Over the years, she has founded a number of charities and donated tens of millions of dollars to causes she believes in. She has helped build schools and in other ways focused on bettering the lives of children. Through a segment of *The Oprah Winfrey Show* called Oprah's Book Club, she has encouraged literacy among her fans and brought new popularity to many literary classics. She has given an incredible boost to the books, influence, and careers of contemporary writers whose work might otherwise not have become known.

Because of all these activities—and more—Oprah has personally earned many

Robert L. Johnson, the founder of Black Entertainment Television (BET). Like Oprah, he is a groundbreaking African-American media figure and philanthropist.

humanitarian, literacy, and service awards during her career, along with dozens of Emmy Awards and many other broadcasting honors for *The Oprah Winfrey Show*.

Even though Oprah's daily talk show is no longer on the air, she is still considered one of the most influential people in the world. As BBC News put it in 2011, "She has become a household name, cultural phenomenon, and one of the richest people on the planet."

What makes Oprah's story particularly fascinating is that she has achieved all of this against seemingly impossible odds.

Truth or Myth?

When someone is as famous as Oprah, her fans want to know more about her. Because of the demand for as much information as people can get about her, many journalists have interviewed Oprah. There are thousands of articles and TV stories about her. Through all these interviews, her fans have learned about Oprah's childhood, her family, and her early career.

There are also many books written about Oprah. (She has never written her own life story.) One such book, *Oprah: A Biography*, by author Kitty Kelley (shown here at a book signing in Chicago), came out in 2010. Before writing the book, Kitty said she read more than 2,000 articles about Oprah, who declined to be interviewed for the project. Kitty also interviewed hundreds of people who knew Oprah or had some connection with her.

Some of the people Kitty interviewed remembered past events differently than Oprah did. They called into question some of Oprah's memories about her childhood, in particular. One of Kitty's sources even said the man Oprah believes is her father isn't actually her father. Many said that Oprah exaggerated some parts of her past to make it more interesting.

Memory and truth are tricky things, though. Different people view, interpret, and remember things differently. Sometimes, memories change over time. That means that two versions of the same event might be dramatically different. Who is to say which version is correct?

Chapter 2
Rocky Road to Success

Today, the world knows her by just one name—Oprah. But when she was born, she was given a slightly different name. She was called Orpah, after a biblical character in the Book of Ruth. "My Aunt Ida had chosen the name," said Oprah many years later, "but nobody really knew how to spell it. So it went down as 'Orpah' on my birth certificate, but people didn't know how to pronounce it. So they put the 'P' before the 'R' in every place else other than the birth certificate. On the birth certificate it is 'Orpah,' but then it got translated to 'Oprah,' so here we are." The revised name stuck, and the little girl became Oprah.

The Little Preacher

Oprah Winfrey was born on January 29, 1954, on the outskirts of Kosciusko, Mississippi. That's a rural town about 70 miles (113 kilometers) northeast of the state capital, Jackson. Oprah was the first child of Vernita Lee, who was just 19 years old when her daughter was born.

The Attala County courthouse in Kosciusko, Mississippi, the town in which Oprah was born and spent the first six years of her life.

The Great Migration

In the late 1950s, Oprah Winfrey's mother, Vernita Lee, moved north from rural Mississippi to the city of Milwaukee, Wisconsin. She was one of about five million African Americans who moved from the Deep South to states in the Northeast, Midwest, and West from the 1940s to the 1970s. This migration, or movement, of African Americans was called the Second Great Migration.

The first Great Migration happened between 1910 and 1930, when black Americans were recruited from the South to work in factories and to help build railroads in the nation's North. Most of those jobs were wiped out by the Great Depression, which was the worldwide economic collapse of the 1930s.

Things turned around in the 1940s and another Great Migration began, with another great wave of African Americans moving to cities to find work. Another reason they left their rural homes was to escape the terrible racism of the Deep South.

African-American artist Jacob Lawrence painted a series of 60 pictures entitled, collectively, "The Migration of the Negro." Taken together, the paintings form a narrative depicting what The New York Times *described as "the shift of African-American populations from a poor and repressive rural South to a prosperous but unwelcoming urban North." This panel provides an impression of masses of people crowding together to head north during what first came to be called the Great Migration in the years before and after World War I.*

By the time Oprah came into the world, Vernita and the child's father, Vern Winfrey, a military man, had already split up.

When Oprah was a little girl, Vernita moved north to Milwaukee, Wisconsin, to find work and make a better life for herself. She did not take Oprah with her. Vernita got a job as a maid, but her lifestyle was not suitable for raising a child. She lived in poverty in a boarding house in a dangerous part of town, and she was rarely home.

Oprah spent the first six years of her life on the family farm with her grandparents, Hattie Mae and Earless Lee. She had no other children to play with, so the farm animals became her friends. She even staged little plays, giving roles to the animals.

Oprah and her grandparents were poor and lived in a house with no running water, indoor bathroom, or electricity. Oprah rarely had new clothes or toys.

Her grandparents were not loving and affectionate with the little girl. In fact, they were just the opposite—they were strict and stern, and they punished her often. Oprah said she was whipped nearly every day. If she misbehaved or didn't finish her chores, her grandmother would hit her, she reported.

Despite this abuse, Oprah credits Hattie Mae with giving her "the foundation for success" that she would not have gained had she spent her early years

> *"I was four years old and I remember thinking, ... 'My life won't be like this, it will be better.' And it wasn't from a place of arrogance, it was just a place of knowing that things could be different for me somehow."*
>
> Oprah Winfrey, 1991

What We Know About O

Oprah's grandmother, Hattie Mae, used the Bible to teach Oprah to read.

A church in Kosciusko, Mississippi, near Oprah's birthplace. According to the sign, this may have been where Oprah appeared before her "first audience" when she recited Bible verses as a little girl.

with her mother. "My grandmother taught me to read, and that opened the door to all kinds of possibilities for me," said Oprah. By the time she was three, the little girl was already reciting Bible verses in front of her entire church congregation.

The Big, Bad City

When Oprah was five, her grandfather died. A year later, her grandmother Hattie Mae became ill and was no longer able to look after her little granddaughter. In 1960, six-year-old Oprah was sent to Milwaukee to live with her mother.

When she arrived in the big city, Oprah discovered she had a half-sister, a baby named Patricia, who had been born in 1959. A year later, Vernita gave birth to another baby, a boy named Jeffrey. Vernita had planned to marry the boy's father, but the wedding never happened.

When Jeffrey was born, Vernita moved her little family out of the rooming house where she had been living—a place so tiny that Oprah slept on the back porch. They moved into a small apartment with Vernita's cousin.

Having three young children was too much for Vernita, so in 1962, she sent eight-year-old

A Good Teacher Makes A World of Difference

During this rocky period in Oprah's life, she met the person she called "my greatest inspiration." Mrs. Duncan was Oprah's fourth-grade teacher in Nashville. She was the first person who told Oprah that she was smart. She also told the little girl not to be afraid of letting people know she had brains.

Mrs. Duncan would often stay after school to work with Oprah on her assignments, to help her choose challenging books to read, and to help the young girl be the best she could be. "For the first time, I believed that I could do almost anything," said Oprah.

Oprah was so inspired by Mrs. Duncan, she decided at the time that she would become a fourth-grade teacher so she could help other children the way Mrs. Duncan had helped her.

Of course, Oprah became a talk show host instead. In 1989, *The Oprah Winfrey Show* presented an episode about inspirational teachers. "My producers surprised me by bringing in Mrs. Duncan as a guest on the show," remembered Oprah. "I hadn't seen her since grade school, and suddenly, I'm reading [from] the teleprompter 'Welcome, Mary Duncan.'"

When Oprah realized that she had just introduced her beloved teacher, she burst into tears on national television. "After all these years, I could say thank you to a woman who had a powerful impact on my early life."

From the age of six on, Oprah's childhood was mostly a tale of two cities: Milwaukee (left), where her mother and half-siblings lived; and Nashville (right), where her father and stepmother lived.

Oprah to Nashville, Tennessee, to live with her father Vernon and enter the fourth grade at school. "That was the beginning of shuttling her back and forth between my house in Nashville and her mother's house in Milwaukee," said Oprah's father.

By this time, Vern was married to a woman named Zelma, and he worked as a janitor at the local university. Vern and Zelma were strict but kind parents to Oprah. They helped her with schoolwork, made sure she had books to read, and took her to church every Sunday.

In 1963, after a year with Vern and Zelma, Oprah went back to live with her mother in Milwaukee. Vernita wanted all her children with her. She promised that she and the kids would finally be a "real family."

What Oprah didn't know at the time—something she found out almost 50 years later—was that during the year she lived with Vern and Zelma, her mother had given birth to another daughter, in April 1963. Vernita had immediately given the baby up for adoption. "I made the decision to give her up because I wasn't able to take care of her," said Vernita in 2011. She said she never told Oprah "because I thought it was a terrible thing ... that I'd done, to give up my daughter when she was born."

Siblings and Secrets

Growing up, Oprah had a half-sister named Patricia and a half-brother named Jeffrey. Both were born in Milwaukee—Patricia in April 1959, Jeffrey in December 1960.

In 1990, Patricia, who was known to struggle with drug addiction, sold a story about Oprah to a tabloid newspaper, causing a falling out between the sisters. The *National Enquirer* gave Patricia $19,000 for spilling Oprah's secrets. Patricia died in February 2003 at age 43. Her death is believed to have been drug-related.

Oprah's brother Jeffrey died in 1989 of AIDS-related illness. He and Oprah also had a strained relationship. Just before his death, Jeffrey told the *National Enquirer* that he and Oprah weren't speaking. He said he felt abandoned by his wealthy half-sister, who did not approve of his lifestyle. Oprah has never talked about the source of their differences.

In the fall of 2010, Oprah found out that she had a *third* half-sibling, also born in Milwaukee, in 1963. This was news that "shook me to my core," she said. A few months later, in January 2011, Oprah introduced to the world on her TV show her newfound half-sister, also named Patricia.

Patricia, who was named after Vernita had given her up for adoption, spent seven years in foster care before she was adopted. Through some 21st-century detective work—by herself and her two children—Patricia found Vernita, her biological mother, and learned that she and Oprah were siblings.

Today, Patricia and Oprah remain close. In 2014, Oprah even bought her half-sister a half-million-dollar house in Wisconsin.

Oprah's Darkest Days

For the next five years, from the time she was 9 until she was 14, Oprah lived with her mother in the tough inner city of Milwaukee. It was a dark, lonely time for the girl. Vernita worked long hours cleaning houses, and she had an active social life, going out with lots of different men in the evenings. Oprah and her siblings were often left at home with babysitters. During those years, Oprah was repeatedly sexually abused.

The first incident happened when Oprah was just nine. A 19-year-old cousin raped her while he was supposedly looking after the children.

He told Oprah not to tell anyone. She kept the secret for more than 20 years. That cousin, along with an uncle and family friends, assaulted Oprah time and time again over the next few years.

Oprah had no self-confidence. Abuse had taught her that sexual activity would get the attention of boys. The young girl mistook that kind of negative attention for the affection she longed for. She began having sexual relationships with a number of partners.

Oprah started getting into trouble at school and stealing from her mother. Eventually, she ran away from her mother's home.

When Oprah was 14, Vernita could no longer handle her eldest daughter. She wanted the girl out of the house, and at one point she tried to send Oprah to a juvenile detention center for troubled kids. Oprah was denied admission to the center, however, because all the beds were filled.

In the summer of 1968, Vernita once again

Culture Shock in Her Own Hometown

In 1967, during her troubled early teenage years in Milwaukee, Oprah was a student at Lincoln High School, a virtually all-black junior-senior high school near downtown Milwaukee.

At the time, a teacher named Gene Abrams was looking for promising African-American kids who might benefit from a new program, called Upward Bound, which gave disadvantaged students a better chance of getting into college. Mr. Abrams had noticed that Oprah spent a lot of time reading by herself in the school cafeteria at lunchtime. The more he got to know her, the more she impressed him with her seriousness and sense of curiosity.

In the late 1960s, Milwaukee was in the process of racially integrating its schools. A virtually all-white suburban school, Nicolet High School, was trying to come up with a list of kids from Milwaukee who might transfer to Nicolet.

Mr. Abrams made sure that Oprah was on that list. Before she knew it, she was about to play a completely unexpected role in her life—helping to integrate Milwaukee-area schools by commuting from the inner city to a suburban school that was overwhelmingly white. Both the commute on city buses and her exposure to suburban kids were harsh reminders of how different her life was from that of her new schoolmates.

When Oprah went to this Milwaukee school, it was Lincoln High School. Today this building is home to a middle school called Lincoln Center of the Arts.

"I remember ... taking the bus with the maids ... who worked out in the suburbs. And there'd be little old me and all the maids with their little bags. It was culture shock for me. It was the first time I realized I was poor. But it made a major difference in my life. Just a major *difference."*

Even though she felt like an outsider, Oprah never felt mistreated or disliked. At times, in fact, she has said that she felt as though she was something of an object of curiosity for her new friends in the North Shore suburbs. "In 1968 it was real hip to know a black person, so I was very popular." She later told Mr. Abrams, about his helping her go to Nicolet, that even with the painful contrasts between the suburbs and her home in the city, and perhaps *because* of them, "You will never know how that changed my life."

A yearbook picture of Oprah from Lincoln High School, taken in the 1960s.

Nicolet High School, in the Milwaukee suburb of Glendale. Years after transferring from Lincoln to Nicolet, Oprah thought of the experience as positive. She also described it as a "culture shock," not as much about race as about realizing how poor she was.

Oprah and her mother, Vernita Lee, pictured together at an event at Walt Disney World in Orlando, Florida, in 1994. The two had a rocky relationship through most of Oprah's childhood.

sent Oprah to live with Vern and Zelma in Nashville—this time for good.

A few years earlier, Vern had opened a barbershop and a small grocery store. Oprah began working for him at the store. Vern and Zelma made her do chores and homework. They insisted she dress "like a proper young lady," stop wearing heavy eye make-up, and stay away from boys.

She had rules to follow. She had a curfew. "She didn't have to like [the rules]," said Vern. "She just had to obey them. 'If you run away, stay away.' That's what I told her. You have

to behave. Behave as if you want to make something of yourself."

In her father's eyes, Oprah had come to him as an "ill-mannered," out-of-control teenager. He and Zelma were tough on the teen, but their goal was to help her turn her life around.

What Vern and Zelma didn't know at this point, though, was that 14-year-old Oprah was pregnant.

What We Know About O

In the fall of 1968, Oprah started attending East Nashville High School, shown here as part of East Nashville Magnet School, a combined middle school and high school. She was one of the first African-American students ever to go to this school.

Chapter 3
Becoming Oprah

Shortly after 14-year-old Oprah confessed to her father and stepmother that she was pregnant, she went into labor. She gave birth to a baby boy—two months early. The stress of telling her parents about the pregnancy was considered the cause of the baby's early arrival. Sadly, the child, who was born around the time of Oprah's 15th birthday, died a few weeks later. "When that child died, my father said to me, 'This is your second chance. This is your opportunity … to make something of your life.'" Oprah took his words to heart and decided it was time to turn her life around.

New Beginnings

Oprah returned to school after the birth of her baby, determined to make the most of the second chance she felt she had been given. She had hidden the pregnancy so well that none of her classmates even knew she had been pregnant. It was a secret Oprah kept for 22 years, until her half-sister sold the story of the baby to a gossip magazine in 1990.

For Vern and Zelma, education had always been a priority. They knew their daughter was intelligent and capable of doing well at school. They wouldn't accept anything less than "A" grades from her. This tough love was just what Oprah needed to succeed. She learned that

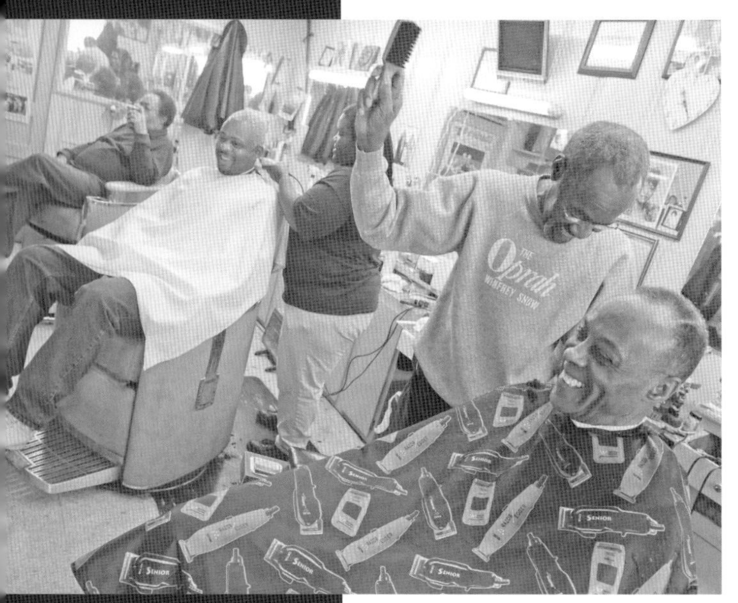

Oprah's father, Vern Winfrey (second from the right, wearing an Oprah Winfrey Show *sweatshirt.) He is shown making a living in 2008, much as he did when Oprah was a teenager living with him in Nashville in the 1960s and 1970s—cutting hair in his own barbershop.*

someone cared enough about her to push her to be the best she could be.

Under Vern and Zelma's guidance, Oprah's life began to change for the better. Going to live with her father was "my saving grace," she said later.

Oprah became an honors student and an active member of her church. As she had done as a little girl in Kosciusko, she started doing Bible readings, reciting sermons, and performing dramatic presentations for her church congregation.

Word of the teenager's talent as a spellbinding speaker spread throughout Nashville. Other congregations invited her to appear at their churches. "I've spoken at every church in Nashville at some point in my life," said Oprah. "You sort of get known for that. Other people were known for singing; I was known for talking."

Oprah's reputation as a dynamic orator spread all the way to California. When she was 16, a church in Los Angeles—nearly 2,000 miles (3,219 km) away—invited her to be a guest speaker. While Oprah was in L.A., she visited Hollywood. She was so inspired by the glamour of "Tinseltown" that she came home determined to use her love of words and performing to become an actress.

What We Know About O

Oprah's father only allowed her to watch one hour of television a day.

Oprah joined her high school public-speaking team. In her junior year, she won the state championship contest for her dramatic interpretation of a passage from a book of poems. "It's like winning the Academy Award," she told her school newspaper at the time. A year later, she won the state tournament for a second time.

In her senior year, Oprah was elected vice president of the Student Council and voted Most Popular Girl. Because of her church and school activities, she was also selected to participate in the 1971 White House Conference on Children and Youth, which took place in Colorado.

Upon her return from the conference, local radio station WVOL interviewed her about the experience. Soon after that, the station sponsored a local beauty pageant called Miss Fire Prevention. A representative from WVOL remembered Oprah and encouraged her to enter the contest.

Although WVOL focused on music and subjects of interest to the black community, Oprah was the only African American in the competition. She didn't think she had a chance of winning—so she had a bit of fun with it.

When contest judges asked Oprah what she wanted to do with her life, she didn't give the same "teacher" or "nurse" answers the other contestants gave. Instead, "I said I wanted to be a broadcast journalist because I believed in the truth. I was interested in proclaiming the truth to the world."

When they asked what she would do if someone handed her a million dollars, she gave another surprise answer: "I'd be a spending fool!" With that, everyone laughed—and Oprah won the competition!

When she went to the radio station to pick up her prize, "they said, 'Would you like to hear your voice on tape?' just sort of as a little treat for me... And I started to read. Now I've been reading since I was three. They couldn't believe how well I read... Before I knew it, there were four guys standing in the room listening to me read."

The people at the radio station were so impressed with Oprah's natural on-air ability that they offered her a part-time job reading the news after school. Oprah worked at WVOL for three years, until a local TV station came calling.

What We Know About O

In 1972, Oprah won two more beauty pageants. First, she was named Miss Black Nashville, then Miss Black Tennessee. She also competed in the national Miss Black America contest, but did not win.

Talking for a Living

After Oprah graduated from high school in 1971, she wanted to go to a university away from Nashville, mainly to escape her father's rules. Vern insisted his daughter stay at home, though. So Oprah enrolled in Speech Communications and Performing Arts at Tennessee State University in Nashville.

In her second year at college, Oprah received a phone call from Chris Clark, the news director of a local television station. He had heard Oprah on radio and thought she would be a perfect TV news anchor. He asked the 19-year-old if she would be interested in working in TV.

"What you see in Oprah today is what I saw so many years ago," said Chris, who is now retired. "Oprah ... had the magic to communicate on television, and that is natural born. You just can't learn that. You can't

Tennessee State University, where Oprah enrolled following her high school graduation in 1971.

develop that. You got it or you don't got it."

Because she was still in school, Oprah turned down Chris's offer three times. She knew that if she took the job, she might never graduate from college. Eventually one of her professors reminded her that the reason people go to school is so they can get a break like the one she was being offered!

"So I went and I interviewed for the job," said Oprah:

"I'd never even been behind the scenes in television... I decided to pretend to be [newswoman] Barbara Walters ... so I sat there, pretending, with Barbara in my head. Did everything I thought she would do. And I was hired. It was amazing."

With that, just before her 20th birthday, Oprah became the youngest news anchor, and the first female African-American news anchor at WLAC-TV (now WTVF) in Nashville.

She knows that part of the reason she got the job was because of her skin color and her gender. Throughout the 1960s, the U.S. government had put together a plan called affirmative action. Under affirmative action, the government and private employers had to hire a certain number of minorities—usually defined as women and people of color—to offset discrimination in hiring practices.

"[WLAC] was trying to fulfill all of [its] quotas and programs," said Oprah. "And so I was hired as a token." Her classmates at Tennessee State, which was primarily African American, teased her because of this. "And I used to say, 'Yeah, but I'm a paid token!'"

Affirmative Action

Women and people of color have historically faced discrimination in the workplace and in schools. This brand of discrimination usually takes a specific form of unfair treatment, such as being denied a job or promotion in the workplace, or admission into a college or university, because of race or gender. In the mid-1960s, mainly through a series of presidential actions known as executive orders and civil rights laws passed by Congress, the U.S. government came up with a plan to help these groups improve their chances for employment and education. This was called affirmative action.

At first, the idea was to make sure people who had been discriminated against in the past, were fairly represented in businesses, colleges, and universities. This was to be accomplished by granting special consideration to women and minorities during the hiring or selection process. In some cases, though, organizations created quotas, meaning that a certain percentage of people hired in a workplace, or accepted into a school or government program, *had* to be women or minorities. People who were hired to meet these quotas were often called "tokens."

In the late 1970s, people began challenging affirmative action, saying it was "reverse discrimination," and it was unfair to white people, particularly white men.

Affirmative action has been controversial since its beginnings. In many states, it has been broadened to address discrimination based not just on race and gender, but religion, sexual orientation, national origin, age, and disability. In other states, affirmative action has been made illegal by lawmakers or statewide vote, and it is still the subject of court cases in the United States.

Oprah was scheduled to graduate from Tennessee State University in 1975. Instead, she made an unexpected decision. She quit school—just one credit shy of earning her degree. After all, her career was already well under way. She was a respected television news anchorwoman.

What We Know About O

Oprah's father was still so strict with her that, even when his daughter was a TV news anchor, she still had a curfew. "I am the 10 o'clock news anchor in Nashville, Tennessee. I am the woman on the newscast reading the news, and my father would say, 'be home by 11.' I'd say, 'Dad, the news is on at 10.' And he goes, 'And it's off at 10:30, so be home at 11.'"

"[Graduating] didn't matter to me, because I was earning a living," she said. "I was on my way. So, I thought, 'I'm going to let this college thing go.'"

By then, Oprah was restless. She was eager to get away from her strict father. She wanted to leave Nashville and move to a bigger city. She

Oprah and her father, Vern Winfrey, are all smiles on the red carpet for an event in 1994. Despite her desire to break away from her father's strict rules, Oprah credits much of the turnaround in her life as a troubled teenager to his insistence that she perform to the best of her capabilities.

was ready to take the next step in her television career, so she started applying for TV jobs in other cities.

One of the applications she sent was for a news anchor position in Baltimore, Maryland—and she got the job. Finally Oprah could spread her wings!

In 1976, at age 22, Oprah moved 700 miles (1,127 km) away from Nashville and started a new job as a news anchor on WJZ-TV.

The WJZ-TV studios in Baltimore. This is where Oprah got her first job in broadcasting outside of Nashville. Originally constructed for WJZ during the early days of television in the late 1940s, it was the first building in Baltimore designed specifically for TV broadcasting.

Oprah's Graduation—12 Years Later

In 1975, Oprah left Tennessee State University, one credit short of graduating. By that point, her TV career was well under way, so she thought she didn't need a degree. "But, my father, from that time on and for years after, was always on my case, because I did not graduate," she said.

In 1987, Tennessee State invited Oprah to speak at a commencement, or graduation, ceremony. At the time, she was hosting her own talk show and had been in a movie, nominated for an Academy Award, and started her own production company. One thing she still hadn't done, though, was graduate from a university.

Oprah felt she couldn't give a commencement speech unless she had a degree. "So I finished my coursework, I turned in my final paper and I got the degree. And my dad was very proud."

Reality Check

Oprah signed a three-year contract and made her debut as co-anchor on the WJZ-TV news in August 1976. "Getting the 6 o'clock news co-anchor job at 22 was such a big deal," she said. "It felt like the biggest deal in the world at the time."

Immediately, though, Oprah faced a number of obstacles. The first was her co-anchor, a veteran news reporter named Jerry Turner. He did not want to share

TV anchor Jerry Turner, shown here in 1980, was a fixture at WJZ-TV when Oprah arrived on the scene in 1976. His resistance to sharing the anchoring duties made her miserable.

What We Know About O

Before Oprah arrived in Baltimore, WJZ-TV launched a campaign to get people excited and curious about this new young anchorwoman. Promos and advertisements said, "What's an Oprah?" The idea was to create interest. Instead, it was a "childish" campaign that embarrassed Oprah. "The whole thing backfired," she said.

his anchor desk with anyone, especially not an inexperienced young woman. Oprah said he made her life miserable every chance he got. "He didn't want me there. I was young. I wasn't just green behind the ears—I had cornstalks growing back there."

The second obstacle Oprah faced was that she didn't fit the image of the "typical" news anchorwoman of the day. At one point, station managers sent her to a hair salon to change her look. The stylist gave Oprah a perm, but left the chemicals in her hair too long. "After a few days, all my hair fell out and I had to shave my head. And then," she laughed, "they *really* didn't like the way I looked, 'cause now I am black and bald and sitting on TV. Not a pretty picture."

The third strike against Oprah was that she was simply not a good news anchor.

She mispronounced words. One time, for example, she called Canada "ca-NAH-da."

She also became emotionally involved in the stories she was covering. "I'd cover a fire and then I'd go back and I'd try to give the victims blankets. And I wouldn't be able to sleep at night because of all the things I was covering during the day."

She also liked to ad lib instead of reading the words as they appeared on the teleprompter. She would add her own comments about a story. She would smile or laugh at a happy story and cry when relating a sad one. News anchors need to keep a poker face when they're on-air—but Oprah couldn't do it. "I was too emotional."

Just eight months after hiring her, WJZ-TV was ready to fire the young newscaster. Because Oprah was on a three-year contract, however, they couldn't do that—but they could assign her to lesser tasks in the newsroom. They removed

Oprah's Idol, Barbara Walters

When Oprah was starting out as a news anchorwoman, she fashioned herself after Barbara Walters, the first female network news anchor in the United States. Oprah's goal was to become "the black Barbara Walters."

Barbara was born in 1929. She started in broadcasting in 1962, doing "women's-interest stories" on NBC's *The Today Show*. In 1974, she became the show's co-host, the nation's first female to hold such a title. Two years later, Barbara became the country's first female co-anchor of a network newscast when she joined the anchor desk of the *ABC Evening News.*

For 25 years, until 2004, Barbara co-hosted the news magazine show *20/20.* For decades, she hosted the occasional *Barbara Walters Special*, in which she interviewed superstar actors, politicians, sports figures, and other international newsmakers. She created and co-hosted *The View* for seven years, until she retired from broadcasting in 2014.

Broadcast legends Barbara Walters and Oprah Winfrey at a New York charity event in 2006.

Oprah's BFF

In 1976, when Oprah was the news anchor at WJZ-TV in Baltimore, she met a production assistant named Gayle King. One night, during a raging snowstorm, Gayle couldn't get home. She ended up spending the night at Oprah's place, where the two 20-somethings talked, gossiped, and bonded. They've been best friends ever since.

The two women talk on the phone every day, they go to parties together, and they go on vacations together. Oprah is godmother to Gayle's two grown children. Because Oprah has never married, and because she and Gayle are so close, some people suggest they are actually a couple. Both women say this is not true, and in the August 2006 issue of her magazine *O, The Oprah Magazine*, she had this to say about the subject:

> *"I understand why people think we're gay.... There isn't a definition in our culture for this kind of bond between women. So I get why people have to label it—how can you be this close without it being sexual?... I've told nearly everything there is to tell. All my stuff is out there. People think I'd be so ashamed of being gay that I wouldn't admit it? Oh, please."*

Oprah and her good friend Gayle King drop in on a fashion show in 2002, about three years after Gayle left TV to become an editor for O, The Oprah Magazine.

Two years after she met Oprah, Gayle left Baltimore to start her own on-camera TV career. She became an award-winning news anchor, reporter, and talk show host. In 1999, she left television to become an editor for *O*. In 2006, she launched *The Gayle King Show* on Oprah's radio station. Five years later, the show moved to Oprah's specialty station, OWN TV.

In the fall of 2011, Gayle became co-host of *CBS This Morning*, a live news and interview program broadcast from New York City.

her from the anchor desk and put her on the early, early morning shift, where she presented short news updates. They made her a weekend reporter doing the stories nobody else wanted to cover. Oprah also wrote news scripts, something she had no talent for.

"It was a horrible demotion," said Oprah, who started using food as comfort. Around this time, she visited her first diet doctor, who put her on a low-calorie food program. "In less than two weeks, I had lost ten pounds," she said. "Two months later, I'd regained 12. Thus began the cycle of discontent, the struggle with my body. With myself."

A Push in the Right Direction

A few months after Oprah was demoted from the news desk, WJZ-TV hired a new general manager. His task was to add some pizzazz to the station, which had recently slipped in the ratings.

He decided that something the station needed was a local talk show. He had met Oprah, but it was his wife who suggested making Oprah one of the new show's hosts. "There is something magical about her," the woman told her husband. "She wears her heart on her sleeve,

> *"What she lacks in journalistic toughness, she makes up for in plainspoken curiosity, robust humor and, above all, empathy... It is the talk show as a group therapy session."*
>
> *Time* magazine, 1988

and she is not at all pretentious [showy].”

The problem was, Oprah didn’t want the job. She begged not to have to do it. She worried that she wouldn’t be taken seriously if she worked on a talk show. Eventually, the general manager convinced a sobbing Oprah to try it out.

On August 14, 1978, Oprah Winfrey began cohosting *People are Talking*. Her on-air partner was an experienced reporter named Richard Sher. The two of them worked perfectly together. They had good chemistry between them, they liked each other, and they encouraged each other.

This photo of Oprah at WJZ-TV in Baltimore was taken in 1978, between her stint on the news desk and her cohosting People are Talking.

For Oprah, the launch of *People are Talking* was a life-changing event. “The moment I sat on the talk show interviewing [my first guest] the Carvel Ice Cream Man [with] his multiple flavors, I knew that I had found home for myself,” she said. “From that first day, I knew instantly this is what I was supposed to do.”

Oprah’s audience also recognized that this was what she was supposed to do. The reviews for this refreshing new host were immediately positive. She was fun, funny, chatty, and interested in her guests. Before long, *People are Talking* was drawing a bigger audience in Baltimore than the top-rated, nationally broadcast *Phil Donahue Show*, hosted by the man considered to be “the king of talk.”

People were talking about Oprah!

After five years with *People are Talking*, Oprah once again grew restless. She was ready for another change. When one of her colleagues moved to Chicago to work on a show called *A.M. Chicago*, she suggested Oprah move there, too. At the time, *A.M. Chicago* was a low-rated, half-hour show—and it needed a new host. Oprah's producer friend encouraged Oprah to apply for the position. She did, and she got the job.

Within a month of Oprah moving into the host's chair, *A.M. Chicago* jumped from last place to first in the ratings. Oprah was now beating Phil Donohue at his own game in his own town!

A year later, *A.M. Chicago* was extended to one hour and renamed *The Oprah Winfrey Show*. A year after that, *The Oprah Winfrey Show* began to be broadcast nationally, on 138 stations around the country. It immediately bumped *The Phil Donahue Show* out of its top spot and became the nation's number-one talk show.

At age 32, Oprah had found her purpose in life.

"Oprah Winfrey is sharper than Donahue, wittier, more genuine, and far better attuned to her audience, if not the world."

Newsday, late 1980s

The King of Talk

Phil Donahue is considered the creator of the modern talk show. Born in 1935, he started his broadcast career in radio in 1957, moving into TV a few years later. He launched *The Phil Donahue Show* in Dayton, Ohio, in 1967. It was the first talk show that focused on issues, rather than celebrities. Phil was also the first talk show host to invite audience participation.

His show was geared toward "women who think," and was so popular that, after two years, it began airing across the country. In 1974, Phil moved the show to Chicago, and 10 years after that, to New York City. The final episode of *Donahue* aired in September 1996, after 29 years on the air. It remains the longest-running syndicated talk show in American television history.

Phil Donahue inspired many future talk show hosts, including Oprah. She once said, "If there hadn't been a Phil, there wouldn't have been a me."

In 1992, Phil Donahue celebrated the 25th anniversary of his pioneering talk show with a special on NBC. On hand to honor "the king of talk" was a legion of TV hosts and personalities, some of them still familiar today. They included, back row, from left: Faith Daniels, Oprah Winfrey, Jerry Springer, Jenny Jones, Montel Williams, Geraldo Rivera; and front row, from left: Sally Jessy Raphael, Larry King, Dr. Ruth Westheimer, Phil Donahue, and Maury Povich.

Chapter 4
The Queen of Daytime TV

A photo of Oprah taken on August 21, 1986, just a couple of weeks before the first *Oprah Winfrey Show* went national on September 8.

The first nationwide episode of *The Oprah Winfrey Show* aired on September 8, 1986. In the beginning, the show was considered tabloid TV. That meant it focused on scandalous, strange, or controversial subjects—and Oprah's fans loved it. By the end of the first year, about 10 million people were watching every day. Oprah was a multi-millionaire and a genuine celebrity. And she was just getting started!

What Audiences Want

The subject of discussion on the first *Oprah* show was "How to Marry the Man or Woman of Your Choice." As the show developed in its early years, the "tabloid TV" label became ever more apparent. Oprah tackled such heated topics as interracial marriages, young men who love older women, and parents who leave their children home alone. She interviewed a convicted killer, housewives who were also prostitutes, and "women who are allergic to their husbands." Guests included devil worshipers, racist skinheads, and self-described witches. These early shows were intended to generate reactions of anger, shock, sadness, and other strong emotions from the audience.

For example, in February 1987, Oprah took her show to Cumming, Georgia. About 35 miles (56 km) north of Atlanta, Cumming and surrounding Forsyth County had a history of violence between blacks and whites dating back to the early 20th century. One of the most dangerous places for black people in the nation, Forsyth was a county where virtually no African Americans had lived for 75 years. It had, in Oprah's own words, "gained the reputation of being a hotbed of racism." In 1987, before Oprah and her show came to Cumming, pro-civil rights blacks and whites had marched to improve race relations. They were met by members of the Ku Klux Klan and other white racists, who hurled rocks and racial slurs at them.

Oprah faced the camera and her audiences in shows that took on tough issues in a "town hall meeting" format.

Set up as a "town hall meeting," Oprah's show was designed to stir up the audience and get people talking. Some of the views expressed on that show were disturbingly unkind toward African Americans. One member of the audience said that when black people moved into his old neighborhood in Atlanta, it turned into "a rat-infested slum area because they don't care.... They don't care." When he sat down, and Oprah asked him to get back up and tell her whether by "they" he meant "they, us, the entire black race," he had this to say: "You have blacks, and you have niggers." When Oprah asked him, "What's the difference between a black person and a nigger to you," he replied:

"I've talked to black people.... They don't want to come up here. They don't want to cause any trouble. That's a black person. A nigger wants to come up here and cause trouble all the time. That's the difference."

There was also, however, a feeling among many white people in the audience that it was time for people to begin talking and living together—as one woman put it, "a time for change ... black and white in Forsyth County. There's no other way." The *Chicago Sun-Times* wrote about the episode, "Oprah served up an hour of sensational television about an explosive issue while generating tons of publicity."

A few months later, she aired a show from the town of Williamson, West Virginia. It was the hometown of a man with AIDS. He had come home to die. People in the town feared him and his illness. The mayor had closed the pool to scrub it clean after the man took a swim there, generating national news headlines. Oprah set up another "town hall meeting," allowing residents to express their feelings about their gay resident. They were not kind to the man. A physician and health official on the show said residents felt the way they did about the young man because they were afraid. But another person in the audience declared, "I am not afraid.... I am repulsed by the man's lifestyle, I am repulsed by his disease, and I am repulsed by him."

O, The Media Owner

In 1986, Oprah created a production company called Harpo Productions. "Harpo" is "Oprah" spelled backward. With that, she became the third woman in the history of the American entertainment industry to own (or co-own) her own studio. Silent film star Mary Pickford was the first in 1919, followed by comedian Lucille Ball in 1950.

In 1988, Harpo Productions became the official owner of *The Oprah Winfrey Show*. Immediately after that, Oprah bought a film production studio in Chicago, which became Harpo Studios. That's where Oprah filmed her talk show until it ended in 2011. The studio has also produced many film and television projects over the years.

In 1998, Oprah co-founded Oxygen Media, a company dedicated to producing cable and Internet programming for women. She and her colleagues sold Oxygen to NBC for $925 million in 2007.

The sign and logo for Harpo Studios, the Chicago home of The Oprah Winfrey Show *from its beginnings in the 1980s through its final episode in May 2011.*

"The original broadcast was exceptionally powerful and raw, with some of the nastiest, meanest and ugliest comments about people with AIDS I have ever seen broadcast on a mainstream program," wrote author Sean Strub, an AIDS survivor and supporter of rights for people with AIDS. Still, millions of people watched this episode. It would be one of many where Oprah tried, as she said in an interview 20 years later, to "tell the stories of the people who had AIDS and ... to put a face on AIDS."

The Oprah Winfrey Show was a safe place where people voluntarily came to confess their sins, to cry, to argue, and to air their dirty laundry.

Oprah didn't just expose other people's secrets on her show, though. She also revealed surprising truths about herself on the air.

For a November 1986 episode, Oprah brought together a group of sexual assault victims and their molesters. During that program, she revealed that she had been raped and repeatedly sexually abused as a child.

In 1989, Oprah introduced her boyfriend, Stedman Graham, to her audience during a show about the difficulties of relationships lived in the public eye. The couple answered questions from the audience and discussed life-in-the-spotlight together. "I love her and she loves me," Stedman told the audience. "She's my woman, and I'm her man."

In 1995, Oprah admitted, on her show, that she had done drugs, specifically crack cocaine.

Oprah also shared her body-image issues with her audiences over the years, as her

Oprah's Steady, Stedman

Since 1986, Stedman Graham has been Oprah's boyfriend, her "life partner," as she calls him. The two met at a charity event, became friends, and started dating two years later. They got engaged in 1992, planned to marry in 1993, but called the wedding off. Today, they live together but have no intention of marrying. "I'm not a traditional woman, and I haven't had a traditional life," said Oprah in 2013. "I think that had Stedman and I gotten married, we certainly wouldn't have stayed married."

A former military man, prison guard, and part-time model and basketball player, Oprah's "six-feet-six of terrific" founded an organization called Athletes Against Drugs in 1985. Today, he is a motivational speaker, author, and educator who runs a marketing-and-consulting firm. He is best known, though, as Oprah's boyfriend.

Because Oprah is such a public figure, her relationship with Stedman has been the subject of gossip, jokes, and tabloid stories for years.

Oprah Winfrey and Stedman Graham at the 1998 premiere of Oprah's movie Beloved.

weight rose and fell like a yo-yo. In November 1988, this personal struggle made for one of Oprah's most memorable shows.

That day, she took to the stage wearing an oversized coat. Dramatically, she whipped off the coat, revealing her new, surprisingly tiny, size-10 self.

Then she wheeled across the stage a wagon filled with 67 pounds (30 kilograms) of animal

The Ups and Downs of Oprah

Since she first started using food for comfort in the 1970s, Oprah has struggled with her weight. In 1992, after gaining and losing weight over and over again, she hired a personal trainer to help her learn to exercise properly. She began jogging and weightlifting. In 1994, she was so healthy that she ran a 26-mile (42-km) marathon!

Oprah managed to stay fit and maintain a healthy weight for many years, but eventually, the pounds started creeping back. In 2008, she admitted in *O, The Oprah Magazine*, that she weighed 200 pounds (91 kg). "I'm mad at myself," she wrote. "I'm embarrassed. I can't believe that after all these years, all the things I know how to do, I'm still talking about my weight."

At that point, she made a new commitment—not to be thin, but to be "strong, healthy, and fit." Since then, she has lost and gained weight again. In 2014, Oprah acknowledged that she still struggles with "the whole weight thing."

Oprah has been criticized for her yo-yo dieting and her focus on her weight. Some critics have said that that makes her an unhealthy role model.

fat. That's how much weight she had lost in the previous five months on a liquid diet. It was no secret to Oprah's fans that she was losing weight, but this was a pretty icky way of showing it. Some have said that it also played into the popular media's glorifying of "perfect" female body types, which can encourage risky health habits and lead to feelings of low self-esteem.

Later, Oprah called this moment her greatest on-air regret. It was a "big, big, big, big, big, big, big mistake," she said. She came to realize that losing the weight the way she did was dangerous and set a bad example for her viewers. In addition, she quickly gained back the weight she had lost.

She also called the reveal of her thinner body "one of the biggest ego trips of my life."

Oprah shows off her new figure and dramatically reveals her weight loss with a wagon filled with 67 pounds (30 kg) of animal fat. Her stated goal was "to get into that pair of size 10 Calvin Klein jeans. Two hours after the show, I started eating to celebrate ... [and] of course, within two days those jeans no longer fit!"

A Change of Heart

In the 1991–1992 television season, the audience for *The Oprah Winfrey Show* reached its absolute peak, with about 13 million American viewers tuning in every day. The majority of viewers were middle-aged, middle-class, white women. Because of its varied and intriguing subjects, though, the show also appealed to men and people of different races, ethnicities, and ages.

Of course, some shows drew more attention than others.

On February 10, 1993, *Oprah* drew one of its largest audiences ever. That day, Oprah interviewed superstar Michael Jackson in his California home at Neverland Ranch. It was the first time in 14 years the King of Pop had allowed anyone to interview him.

With Oprah, he talked about being abused as a child, about his plastic surgeries, about the condition that made his skin lighten, and why he grabbed his crotch during performances. He said he did not do it on purpose and explained, "... if I'm doing a movement and I go 'BAM' and I grab myself, it's the music that compels me to

For the Kids

In 1991, Oprah pushed for a new law to help protect abused children. She testified in front of a U.S. Senate committee that was considering enacting the law, telling her own painful story of childhood abuse. She asked members of Congress to establish the National Child Protection Act to create a national database of convicted child abusers. In 1993, President Bill Clinton signed what had become known as "the Oprah bill," and the National Child Protection Act became law.

In the 1990s, Oprah began campaigning on behalf of abused children, both on her show and in Washington, D.C., among members of Congress. This photo, taken in November 1994, shows Oprah consoling a member of a local church in South Carolina who is distressed over the drowning of two little boys by their mother, Susan Smith. Billed as a "town hall meeting," this show was one of many where Oprah addressed issues related to child abuse.

do it ... [and] I'm a slave to the rhythm."

Up to 90 million people around the world watched the live show. It remains the most-watched interview in TV history. "It was the most exciting interview I had ever done," said Oprah. She also called it her "finest hour in television."

Time magazine described the event: "Part grand Oprah, part soap Oprah, the ... show was at the very least great TV: live, reckless, emotionally naked."

Oprah poses with pop icon Michael Jackson about a month before his memorable interview on her show in February 1993.

By the mid-1990s, talk TV, in general, had become more reckless and trashy—and Oprah was tired. Two particular interviews led her to question the messages her show was sending to her millions of viewers every day.

The first was an interview with members of the racist Ku Klux Klan. After that episode aired, Oprah realized that the organization had used its exposure on her national show to attract new members. She felt used and angry.

The second show that led Oprah to question her show's purpose brought together husbands and wives—and the husbands' girlfriends. During that show, one of the men announced that his mistress was pregnant. Oprah said the look of shock and humiliation on the man's wife's face broke her heart. She felt ashamed that she had participated in the woman's public embarrassment.

WHAT WE KNOW ABOUT O

In 1987, Oprah won her first Daytime Emmy Award for Outstanding Talk Show Host. It was the first of more than 40 Daytime Emmys *The Oprah Winfrey Show* would earn in various categories. In 1998, Emmy honored Oprah with a Lifetime Achievement Award. The following year, she took herself (and in 2000, her show) out of the running for any future Emmy Awards. "After you've achieved it for a lifetime, what else is there?" she said at the time.

As a result of these two episodes, Oprah changed her show's focus in 1994. She steered away from tacky, gossipy subjects, in favor of positive stories about health, self-help, good people, and good news. "I will only allow my [show] to be used as a force for good," she said.

With this change of attitude, though, came an immediate drop in ratings for *The Oprah Winfrey Show*. Audience numbers eventually bounced back up, but they never again reached the height of the 1991–1992 season. For the rest of the program's lifetime, it consistently drew more than seven million fans each day. More important to Oprah, though, was that with her move away from tabloid TV, she gained the respect and trust of her loyal fans.

In September 1996, in her efforts to use her show for good, Oprah launched a book club. For the next 15 years, several times a year, Oprah would recommend a book for her viewers to read and discuss. The first-ever selection for

Jacquelyn Mitchard, author of The Deep End of the Ocean, *the first selection for Oprah's Book Club. The novel, which was selected for the book club in 1996, became a bestseller. In 1999, it was adapted into a movie starring Michelle Pfeiffer, Treat Williams, and Whoopi Goldberg.*

Oprah's Book Club was *The Deep End of the Ocean*, the first novel by author Jacquelyn Mitchard.

Over the years, Oprah highlighted many works by first-time novelists, as well as selections by well-known authors such as Maeve Binchy, Maya Angelou, and Toni Morrison. In its later years, Oprah's Book Club promoted literary classics, including John Steinbeck's *East of Eden* (first published in 1952), Leo Tolstoy's *Anna Karenina* (1870s), and *The Good Earth*, by Pearl S. Buck (1932).

Every book Oprah recommended became an instant bestseller. The sales boost was so huge that Oprah's staff had to give publishers a heads-up, months in advance, when one of their books was to be featured. Publishers needed time to print mass quantities of special Oprah editions, to prepare for a huge sales boost. This dramatic leap in sales—thanks to Oprah's support—became known as "The Oprah Effect."

Oprah and writer Maya Angelou at an awards ceremony in 1996. In addition to bringing Maya's works to the attention of millions of readers on her show, Oprah formed a fast friendship with the renowned poet, right up to the time of Maya's passing away in 2014 at the age of 86.

Too Much Power?

The same year she launched her book club, Oprah also learned that her power over the public could have a downside.

In April 1996, she hosted a show about mad cow disease. The illness was infecting some European—but not American—cattle. When transmitted to humans, the disease was said to

The Oprah Effect

Because Oprah was so influential, any product she promoted on *The Oprah Winfrey Show* instantly became a must-have item. Some companies saw their sales multiply by a factor of 100. That meant, if the company usually sold 10 units of the featured product in a day, it was suddenly selling 1,000 a day after Oprah got her hands on it. That sales boost was called "The Oprah Effect."

After she launched her book club in 1996, the literary world benefited from Oprah's power. Every book selected by Oprah's Book Club instantly shot to the top of bestseller lists, and its author could count on at least a million extra book sales.

If Oprah loved something and talked about it, sales soared. On the other hand, as beef farmers discovered in 1996, anything Oprah didn't like was doomed.

destroy brain tissue and could lead to insanity, or even death.

On Oprah's show, a guest claimed that American farmers were feeding their cattle ground-up meat from European mad cows. Oprah replied, "it has just stopped me cold from eating another burger!"

Immediately, U.S. beef sales tumbled, and cattle prices dropped dramatically.

A group of Texas cattle ranchers sued Oprah. They said they had lost about $12 million in sales after her show, and it was her fault. They said her anti-burger comment—and her influence over millions of people—had damaged their industry.

In early 1998, the lawsuit against Oprah went to court in Amarillo, Texas. For more than a month, she moved her talk show to Amarillo, so she could attend court during the day and tape her show at night. "It was one of the most stressful times I've ever personally experienced," she said.

On February 26, 1998, a judge and jury sided with Oprah, pronouncing her not guilty of defaming, or using her words to harm, the cattle producers. The ranchers appealed the decision, only to lose once and for all in court six years later.

Oprah's Other Lives

By the end of the 20th century, Oprah was a household name. She was one of the wealthiest and most influential women in the world. *The Oprah Winfrey Show* was broadcast in more than 100 nations around the globe. But Oprah

> *"I became obsessed with the book* [The Color Purple]... *I would literally walk around with a backpack filled with books—because I didn't have a book club [in the early 1980s]—and I would just start a conversation with people and say, 'Have you read* The Color Purple?' *And if they hadn't, I'd say, 'Here, have a copy, right here.' I was literally obsessed with it."*
>
> Oprah Winfrey, 2014

was no longer just a talk show host. By now, she was a movie star, a film and TV producer, and a generous philanthropist.

Oprah's film career started in 1985, when she won a starring role in a movie called *The Color Purple*. It was based on Alice Walker's 1982 book of the same name and directed by Steven Spielberg.

Oprah loved the book so much that, when she first read it, she bought every copy she could find in bookstores and gave one to everybody she knew.

The Color Purple documented the struggles with racism, abuse, and poverty faced by African-American women in the early 1900s.

In 1984, when Oprah learned that *The Color Purple* was being made into a movie, "I started praying to be in the movie," she said. She desperately wanted to be part of it, even though she had never before acted in a film.

Acclaimed composer, musician, producer, and entertainment company executive Quincy Jones "discovered" Oprah when he saw her on TV and felt she would be perfect for the role of Sofia in Steven Spielberg's movie The Color Purple. *Quincy and Oprah are shown here at a People's Choice Awards event in 1997.*

Around that time, one of the film's producers, Quincy Jones, happened to be in Chicago and one morning saw Oprah hosting her TV show, *A.M. Chicago*. As soon as Quincy saw Oprah on TV, he knew he had found the perfect person to play the character of Sofia in the film. Sofia was a "fat and feisty" African-American woman who refused to tolerate abuse by others.

Quincy didn't know whether Oprah *could* act, though, so she had to audition, or try out, for the part. At the audition, Oprah proved she could act, and she earned the role of Sofia. She said that working on the film was one of the highlights of her life.

Oprah's performance in *The Color Purple* was so impressive that she was nominated for

Oprah in a scene from The Color Purple, *the 1985 movie that garnered 11 Academy Awards nominations but no wins. Oprah was nominated for Best Actress in a Supporting Role, and she was also nominated for a Golden Globe award in a similar category.*

an Academy Award and a Golden Globe Award. She didn't win either, but her childhood dream of becoming an actress had finally come true.

After *The Color Purple*, Oprah went on to star in a TV movie called *The Women of Brewster Place* (1989). She earned more great reviews for her performance on that project, which was produced by Harpo Studios. On the strength of that, she acted in, and produced, a spin-off TV series called *Brewster Place* (1990). It got such poor reviews that it was canceled after 11 episodes.

Oprah as Mattie Michael in the ABC-TV series Brewster Place. *The show failed to attract the favorable attention achieved by a previously released TV movie called* The Women of Brewster Place.

The Color Snubbed

The Color Purple was nominated for 11 Academy Awards, including Best Supporting Actress for Oprah. Fans and critics were shocked when, come Oscar night, the movie did not win a single award. Oprah "was stunned" by the results.

It is considered one of the biggest "snubs" in Oscar history. Some people have suggested that *The Color Purple* won no awards because of the negative way it portrayed black men. Others believed it was simply because it was "a black movie." Others said it was because members of the Academy didn't like director Steven Spielberg, who had previously directed mostly science-fiction/horror blockbusters, such as *Jaws, Close Encounters of the Third Kind, E.T. the Extra-Terrestrial*, and *Indiana Jones* thrillers.

Whatever the reason, *The Color Purple* is tied with a 1977 movie, *The Turning Point*, for earning the most Oscar nominations without winning a single award.

Over the next few years, Oprah played minor roles in TV and film productions, but it wasn't until 1998 that she played another starring role in a feature film. That year, she played the lead character—a former slave named Sethe—in a movie called *Beloved*. Oprah was also the film's executive producer.

Based on a Toni Morrison novel, *Beloved* was about the impacts slavery had in the United States. It was an absolute flop at the box office. Oprah lost tens of millions of dollars on it.

This rare failure sent Oprah into a dangerous state of depression. In 2011, she described it as "a massive, depressive macaroni-and-cheese-eating tailspin."

It was "the only time in my life I was ever depressed. I recognized I was depressed because I've done enough shows [to know], 'Oh, this is what those people must feel like.'"

Oprah was stung by the negative reaction to the film. It would be 15 years before she took another big-screen leading role.

Oprah and Danny Glover in a scene from the 1998 movie Beloved.

The Church of Oprah

Despite the financial failure of *Beloved*, Oprah moved into the 21st century as one of the wealthiest women in the world. In 2000, she was worth $800 million, making her the richest African American of the 20th century.

Oprah didn't keep all that money for herself, though. Ever since she launched *The Oprah Winfrey Show* nationally in 1986, Oprah had donated money to charities. She favored groups that helped children, abused women, the hungry, and the homeless. She contributed to churches, AIDS organizations, and libraries. Mostly, though, Oprah supported education, through scholarships and direct donations to schools.

In the late 1990s, she folded all of her charitable giving into one new organization, the Oprah Winfrey Foundation. Read to Lead, a national movement that promotes reading to help people better themselves, had these words of praise for Oprah: "... she has awarded hundreds of grants to organizations that support the education and empowerment [the ability to have greater control over one's life] of women, children and families in the United States and around the world." Operating as a "private charity," her foundation received more than $240 million in its first ten years, all of it donated by Oprah herself.

In 1998, she also created Oprah's Angel Network, a charity designed to collect donations from her viewers. Oprah paid all the costs to manage and run this organization, so that 100 percent of her fans' donations went directly to the causes the charity supported.

Oprah visits people from New Orleans being temporarily sheltered in Houston following the devastation of Hurricane Katrina in 2005. Oprah created the Oprah's Angel Network Katrina Homes Registry, which raised more than $15 million dollars for hurricane relief efforts.

Oprah's Angel Network operated for the next 12 years, raising more than $80 million for projects around the world. The Angel Network helped build 60 new schools in 13 different countries, along with women's shelters and homes for youth.

By the close of the 20th century, Oprah was known and admired for her generosity, commitment to inspirational talk-show topics, and open discussion about her personal spiritual journey.

Clearly, she was more than just another superstar celebrity. Millions of people in the United States and around the world now considered her a spiritual leader.

In 2002, *Christianity Today* magazine wrote, "As with a pastor and her parishioners, the bond between Oprah and those in her audience is sacred. She understands the magnitude of the power she wields over them and seems to want to use it to guide them toward better lives."

Not everyone believed in what the magazine called "the Church of O," however. Some considered her brand of "religion" to be nothing more than what some critics called misguided, mystical "baloney." Others thought she held *too* much power over the public.

By this time, Oprah's influence was indeed astounding. She reached millions of people around the world every day through her talk show, her website (oprah.com), her book club, her charities, and her production studio.

By that time, her crowd of critics had also grown. And as Oprah marched into the new century, those critical voices seemed to speak even louder, especially whenever she made a few missteps along the way.

Chapter 5
Oprah in the 21st Century

As Oprah moved into the 21st century, some argued that she was "the world's most powerful woman," "one of the 100 people who most influenced the 20th century," and "America's most powerful black woman." *Life* magazine called her the most influential woman and the most influential black person of her generation. In the early years of the new century, Oprah's name showed up on list after annual list of the most powerful this, the most influential that, the richest one of those. In 2007, *Vanity Fair* magazine wrote that it was conceivable she had "more influence on the culture than any university president, politician, or religious leader, except perhaps the Pope." Political commentator Bill O'Reilly called her "the most powerful woman in the world, not just in America." With great power, though, came great responsibility—and much criticism—for Oprah.

Oprah has made it onto more "most" lists, and for more years running, than most of us could possibly keep track of. According to the Gallup poll's yearly "most-admired" polling, Oprah consistently ranks as one of the most admired women in the world. Her highest ranking came in 2007, when she was tied for first place with then-U.S. Senator Hillary Clinton, shown here with Oprah at an International Emmy Awards Gala in New York City.

A New Audience

With the launch of a new century came the launch of a new project for Oprah. The first issue of *O, The Oprah Magazine* rolled off the presses in April 2000. The 300-page publication flew off shelves so quickly that the publisher immediately had to print hundreds of thousands of extra copies. It was considered the most successful magazine launch in history.

The theme of that first issue, which reached 1.6 million fans, was "Live Your Best Life." Since then, every single issue of *O, The Oprah Magazine* has had a theme, focusing on a particular emotion or lesson—and every single issue has featured a photo of Oprah on the cover. Her words of wisdom appear on the back page in a column called "What I Know for Sure." (A revised and updated collection of the columns over the first 14 years of the magazine's existence was published in 2014.)

Oprah created a South African edition of the magazine in 2002, and from 2004 to 2008, she published another magazine called *O at Home*. Millions of people, mostly women, continue to read *O* every month.

Oprah mugs for the camera as she poses with the first issue of O, The Oprah Magazine *at a launch party in April 2000. The positively themed magazine bears the title for the topic of its first issue, "Live Your Best Life!"*

The Price of Fame

While millions of people around the world adored Oprah, she had also collected her share of critics by the turn of the century. Some called Oprah controlling, self-centered, and materialistic. Others felt Oprah had lost touch with reality, and no longer had anything in common with the majority of her viewers.

Some questioned her ethics when she highlighted unproven medical treatments on her show. "All too often," wrote *Newsweek* magazine, "Oprah winds up putting herself and her trusting audience in the hands of celebrity authors and pop-science artists pitching wonder cures and miracle treatments that are questionable or flat-out wrong, and sometimes dangerous."

As if to prove their points, Oprah's critics jumped on any slip-up she ever made.

For example, in 2004, Oprah gave every member of her studio audience a new car worth more than $28,000. It appeared to be a generous gesture, and the scene when the audience realized that everyone was about to receive a new car was as wild as you can imagine. But as naysayers pointed out, the Pontiacs had been donated by General Motors, and each of the 276 new vehicle owners immediately had to pay $7,000 in taxes, because the cars were considered prizes, not gifts. Many didn't keep the cars because of this.

"Was this really a do-good event Winfrey pulled off," asked a writer in the *Chicago Sun-Times*, "or a cold-blooded publicity stunt?"

The car offering was certainly one of the largest giveaways in the history of *The Oprah*

Winfrey Show, but it wasn't unusual for Oprah to shower her audience members with expensive gifts. At least once a year, beginning in 1999, Oprah presented an episode called "Oprah's Favorite Things." During these shows, which usually aired around Thanksgiving or Christmas, Oprah sent her audiences home with thousands of dollars worth of gifts.

While the audience members loved it, shrieking with delight at their good fortune, Oprah's critics viewed it as over-the-top materialism. Like the cars, all the "Favorite Things" freebies were donated to *The Oprah Winfrey Show* by suppliers and manufacturers thrilled to have their products benefit from Oprah's magic touch.

Oprah's Favorite Things

Beginning in 1999, Oprah presented an annual "Oprah's Favorite Things" episode. On these shows, she gave away a collection of products to all the people lucky enough to be in the audience that day. Over the years, guests took home everything from pie to popcorn, TVs to tote bags, appliances to UGG boots. Gift packages included clothing, jewelry, cosmetics, books, CDs, DVDs, electronics, and housewares. In 2010, Oprah even sent each of her guests on a cruise.

The value of the annual collection of Oprah's Favorite Things ranged from a low of about $700 in 2008 to a high of more than $40,000 in 2010. (In 2009, for reasons never explained, there was no "Favorite Things" episode.)

After each of these giveaway episodes, sales of featured products skyrocketed, sometimes saving struggling businesses, and sometimes overwhelming small companies not set up for dealing with such volume.

More Fuel for Critics

In the late 1990s and early 2000s, *The Oprah Winfrey Show* focused on what Oprah called "Change Your Life Television." That meant she presented shows and guests with uplifting messages, focused on inspirational or spiritual subject matter, and encouraged her audiences to follow their hearts, take responsibility for their lives, and be the best they could be.

Around 2004, though, Oprah began to be criticized because tabloid-style topics started to creep back into her shows.

A 2004 episode called "Is Your Child Leading a Double Life?" focused on the sexual habits and sexual language favored by teenagers. The episode was said to have drawn more than 1,600 complaints from viewers offended by the episode's "obscene" words, "vulgar

Oprah is photographed in January 2004 leaving a 50th birthday celebration in Los Angeles. In the year to come, some of Oprah's shows became the target of criticism from people who felt that her subjects were becoming too sensational or materialistic. One of them was the "You get a car!" extravaganza; another was the episode in which teenage sexuality was discussed in frank terms. As much as these shows invited criticism, they count among some of the most popular Oprah *episodes. Over time, Oprah shifted the focus of her show's contents in an effort to accent more positive, inspiring subjects.*

conversations," and "horrible, horrible filth." The Federal Communications Commission (FCC), the government agency responsible for overseeing television and other media, launched an investigation. Two years later, the FCC ruled that the show was not "indecent," because the discussion was not designed to shock the audience. "Rather," wrote the FCC, "it [was] designed to inform viewers about an important topic."

In the next few years, *The Oprah Winfrey Show* continued to air episodes on inspirational subjects, but also seemed to increase the number of shows on tabloid topics that had shock value or controversy. Oprah fans and haters debated whether these were important discussions about uncomfortable subjects, or sensational displays designed simply to get more viewers.

More and more, celebrities began using Oprah's show as a platform to confess their sins, problems, and secrets. The most famous example of a type of celebrity "confession" on *Oprah* happened in May 2005. On that show, a seemingly alarmed Oprah watched as an out-of-control Tom Cruise jumped up on the sofa, and kneeled severeal times, proclaiming his love for new girlfriend (now ex-wife) Katie Holmes. The incident certainly did not portray Tom very favorably, but in the view of some, it also reflected badly on Oprah and her show.

For her part, Oprah has since spoken out against the overexcited response, which she referred to as a "brouhaha," that was made of the episode.

In an interview, she had this to say about

Never shy when it comes to mocking celebrities, the animated sitcom South Park *had its satirical sights set on Oprah Winfrey and Tom Cruise in this scene from a 2006 episode, which came out in the wake of Tom's "couch-jumping" scene on* Oprah.

Tom and his antics:

> *"He was in love, he was very happy about it, he was on a show, he knew me, he came to play. That was it.... I thought it was an expression of delightful exuberance and being in love."*

And she said this about how the episode was handled in the mainstream and social media:

"I'm not even gonna show it here. You know why? Because I don't want people getting whacked out about it, ... using it out of context, playing it over and over and over again. Because I thought that was really unfair."

Author James Frey in 2003, around the time that his controversial memoir, A Million Little Pieces, *was published.*

Oprah also drew criticism for what some described as her "vicious attack" on author James Frey. In September 2005, Oprah chose his memoir, *A Million Little Pieces*, as her selection for Oprah's Book Club. Four months later, she found out that James had mostly made up some of the specifics in the story about his struggles with drug addiction and recovery.

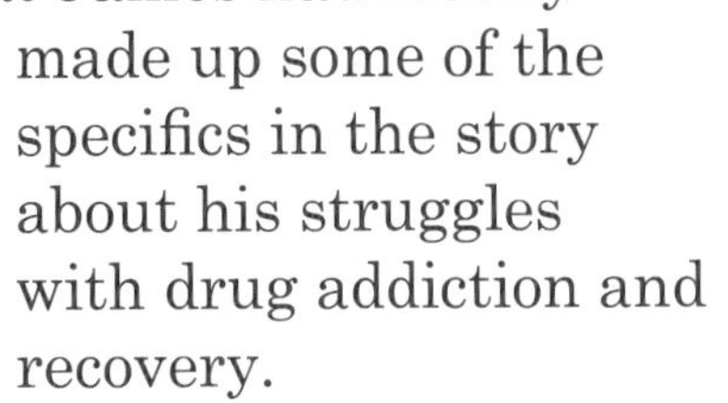

It turned out that much of the story had been exaggerated or invented. Strictly speaking, it wasn't a true-life story after all. By then, however, thanks to Oprah's having featured the book, James had earned millions of dollars in book sales.

In January 2006, Oprah brought James back on her show to confront him about his memoir. "I feel duped," she said during the live

"The amazing thing is that anyone—including Oprah—believed any of Frey's stories once they realized he was trying to manage good sobriety without much [support], because this is a trick very few druggies and alcoholics can manage. I know, because I'm both. Substance abusers lie about everything, and usually do an awesome job of it.... The unstated warning of [Oprah's] cool and methodical dismantling of James Frey seems to have been Embarrass the Book Queen and the Book Queen will get you back double, in front of millions ... and your editor, too."

Author Stephen King

broadcast. "But more importantly, I feel that you betrayed millions of readers." In the eyes of some, that was the day James Frey learned the price of betraying Oprah's trust—public humiliation.

James's well-known publisher and editor, Nan Talese, was also on the show that day, and she took responsibility for publishing the book. Over the months to come, she openly expressed her disapproval of Oprah's treatment of James on the show, calling the interview a "mean and self-serving ... ambush."

The *Washington Post* said it was "a public flogging." Others said Oprah "publicly scolded and humiliated" the author, "shredded him on live TV," and "publicly turned him into road-kill."

In the eyes of many, however, the truth was

that James Frey had partly made up a reality he portrayed as "factual." And Oprah, who had unwittingly participated in this, had the right—some said the duty—to hold him responsible.

Two years later, Oprah phoned James to personally apologize for her harsh behavior. She also apologized for abruptly telling him, just moments before air time, that the show's topic had been changed from a panel discussion with other writers to "The James Frey Controversy." In 2011, she brought him back on her show to publicly apologize for her tough treatment.

For his part, James admitted on the show that he had tried to sell his book as fiction first, but no one would publish it. He said that was when he made a bad decision and began to present it as a memoir.

On Top of the World

While some people consider these episodes to be among Oprah's darkest moments, these particular shows also remain among her most memorable. And no matter how much disapproval anyone ever threw Oprah's way, her fans stood by her, far outnumbering her critics.

Thanks to those fans, *The Oprah Winfrey Show* was the highest-rated talk show on U.S. television every year throughout its lifetime on the airwaves. In an annual poll, Oprah was voted America's favorite TV personality six times between 2000 and 2010. *Forbes* magazine named her most powerful celebrity four times during the same time frame. In 2005, in another poll, the American public named her the greatest woman in American history. In 2010, *Life*

"As much as we can be cynical about a lot of things [Oprah] does, at the end of the day she's done so much for particularly women and African-Americans in this country. If she gets a lot of money as a result of this, she still has created good in the world. The net benefit is to us."

Media critic and analyst Jonathan Gray, quoted in *USA Today*, 2004

magazine included Oprah on the list of the 100 people in history who have changed the world. She was the only living woman on that list.

During the first decade of the 21st century, Oprah was given humanitarian awards, service awards, literary awards, special recognitions, and media awards.

Still, she never stopped working, creating, and growing.

In 2005, Oprah co-produced a Broadway musical based on *The Color Purple*. It played more than two years in New York before going on tour. In January 2015, a new Broadway version was announced. Also to be co-produced by Oprah, the show was due to open in late 2015.

In 2006, Oprah Radio went on the air, broadcasting classic episodes from *The Oprah Winfrey Show*, along with other Oprah-endorsed educational, spiritual, and informational programming.

From 2006 to 2009, Oprah brought to life a

International Inspiration

In 2000, former South African president Nelson Mandela (shown here with Oprah in 2002) visited the United States. While he was in the country, he appeared on *The Oprah Winfrey Show*. "It was the interview of a lifetime," said Oprah.

In his homeland, Nelson had been imprisoned for 27 years because he protested against apartheid. Apartheid was a system of legalized racial segregation and abuse of non-white South Africans. Nelson believed in justice and equality for all.

While he was in jail, Nelson became the face of the anti-apartheid movement. People around the world called for his release and for the end of apartheid.

Nelson was released from prison in 1990. He was president of South Africa from 1994 to 1999.

number of characters in animated films. She voiced Gussy the Goose in *Charlotte's Web*, Judge Bumbleton in *Bee Movie*, and the mother of the princess in *The Princess and the Frog*.

In 2007, she opened a school for girls in South Africa.

Later that same year, Oprah did something

Oprah at a recording session during the making of Charlotte's Web. *Oprah provided the voice characterization of Gussy the Goose (shown at right) in the 2006 live-action/computer-animated movie.*

Oprah's School

Oprah flew to South Africa in 2012 to be on hand for the first graduation ceremony of the Oprah Winfrey Leadership Academy for Girls. Here, she celebrates with members of the graduating class.

In 2000, Oprah pledged to former South African president Nelson Mandela that she would build a school in South Africa. She immediately created a foundation to support the project, and over the next few years, she personally donated more than $40 million to the cause.

The Oprah Winfrey Leadership Academy for Girls opened in 2007, with 152 handpicked students, aged 11 to 13. The girls were chosen because they showed great academic and leadership potential, despite underprivileged backgrounds. Nelson Mandela attended the opening ceremonies.

Within nine months of the school's opening, some of the girls reported sexual and physical abuse by one of the school's dorm matrons. Oprah flew to South Africa to personally apologize to the children and their families. She fired some staff members and changed some of the hiring processes. Two years later, the matron was found not guilty of the abuse charges. The judge in the case ruled that prosecutors had been unable to prove the charges. Some of the students had also contradicted each other and themselves as to when the incidents occurred. Despite being "profoundly disappointed at the outcome of the trial," Oprah declared that she "will forever be proud of the nine girls who testified with the courage and conviction to be heard."

In 2012, the first 72 students graduated from the academy. Today, the school is home to about 300 girls who live in dormitories on the 52-acre (21-hectare) property.

The school features state-of-the-art classrooms and computer, art, and science labs, a theater, a library, and sports facilities.

Oprah joins Barack and Michelle Obama at a December 2007 rally in Manchester, New Hampshire. Oprah threw her support behind Barack Obama in both the race for the 2008 Democratic presidential nomination and the presidential election in November.

she had never done before. She entered the world of politics when she threw her support behind Barack Obama's bid to win the Democratic Party's nomination for president in the upcoming 2008 election.

Many people were surprised that Oprah did not support Barack's main competitor, Hillary Clinton, in the Democratic race. After all, Hillary had appeared on *The Oprah Winfrey Show* many times over the years, and her candidacy would have represented a huge step forward for women in U.S. politics.

Of course, the candidacy of Barack Obama held the promise of great strides forward nationally as well, and his campaign excited many who thought they would never live to see an African American become president of the United States.

"I have great respect for Hillary Clinton," said Oprah. "Because I am for Barack does not mean I am against Hillary or anybody else."

In the end, Barack defeated Hillary to become the Democratic presidential nominee. Researchers estimated that Oprah's support drew as many as 1.6 million votes, pushing him ahead of Hillary in the race leading to the nomination.

Oprah continued to support Barack through the presidential campaign. She was in the audience during his victory speech in Chicago on the night he won the election, November 6, 2008. "It was one of the most electrifying and emotional nights I have ever experienced," she said. A year later, Oprah would experience another highly emotional moment, one that stunned her fans.

The End of the *Oprah* Era

On November 20, 2009, Oprah stood before her studio audience and uttered the words her fans hoped they would never hear. "After much prayer, and months of careful thought, I've decided that next season, season 25, will be the last season of *The Oprah Winfrey Show*," she said through tears.

"This show has been my life, and I love it

What We Know About O

In 2001, the University of Illinois began offering a course called "History 298: Oprah Winfrey, the Tycoon." The University of Redlands in California also teaches a course titled "Oprah: The Woman, The Empire," in its Women's and Gender Studies Department. In 2012, Cornell University, in Ithaca, New York, offered a course called "The Oprah Book Club and African American Literature."

enough to know when it's time to say goodbye. Twenty-five years feels right in my bones, and it feels right in my spirit. It's the perfect number. The *exact* right time."

Oprah announced that the final episode of her show would air in 2011, almost 25 years to the day since she had begun her national broadcast. But that's not to say the Queen of Daytime TV had any intention of *totally* pulling the plug on her television career.

A year earlier, she had announced her plans to launch her own TV network. It was to be called OWN, which stands for the Oprah Winfrey Network, and it would focus on all things Oprah.

At that moment, though, that was little comfort for her loyal viewers, who were stunned by news of the end of their beloved daily *Oprah Winfrey Show*.

Chapter 6
New Directions

On September 13, 2010, Oprah launched her show's 25th—and final—season. The first episode of the season featured actor John Travolta, who had been voted by Oprah's fans as their favorite guest. It was the first of many "Best of Oprah" special episodes that would appear during the show's last months. In mid-April 2011, *The Oprah Winfrey Show* began a 30-day countdown to its grand finale. Many of the final month's episodes featured superstar guests, follow-ups with previous guests, or trips down memory lane. Among Oprah's last visitors were President Barack Obama and First Lady Michelle Obama. Their presence marked the first time a sitting president and first lady had ever appeared together on Oprah's show. The final episode of *The Oprah Winfrey Show* aired on May 25, 2011. It was a surprisingly quiet show with just one guest—Oprah Winfrey.

President Barack Obama and First Lady Michelle Obama are seen in one of the last episodes of The Oprah Winfrey Show *during a taping at Harpo Studios in 2011.*

Oprah Down Under

At the end of the first show of Oprah's farewell season, she announced to her audience that "This is really my last chance to do something really big.... So I started to think about where would I most want to go." After working the members of the audience into an increasingly agitated state with thoughts of return visits to New York and Philadelphia, she finally broke the news—"We're going to Australia!"—over and over again, in the chant that had become a familiar ritual during some of Oprah's more spectacular giveaways.

As the 300 stunned, previously selected "ultimate fans" wildly celebrated their fantastic fortune, the nose of a giant airplane poked through the back of the stage. A Qantas Airways ticket counter (and "agents") appeared out of nowhere, and dozens of people dressed in Australian garb swarmed over the set handing out tiny Australian flags to all.

At the height of the commotion, registered airline pilot and ultimate Oprah fan favorite John Travolta appeared, dressed in a pilot's uniform. He grinned and saluted the goings-on as Oprah announced that he would be their pilot. This was a tears-of-joy event that would easily make most fans' list of best-ever Oprah moments!

The eight-day trip took place in December 2010. During the group's visit, Oprah filmed four special episodes of *The Oprah Winfrey Show*. These episodes, which aired in January 2011, were called "Oprah's Ultimate Australian Adventure." The famous Sydney Opera House was renamed the "Oprah House" during her visit.

Oprah speaks to an audience of 6,000 on December 14, 2010, while taping the first of two shows at the Sydney Opera House in Australia.

Oprah Takes Her Final Bow

The grand finale of *The Oprah Winfrey Show* was broadcast over three days in May 2011. The first two episodes, May 23 and May 24, were star-studded spectacles—exactly what fans would expect for Oprah's send-off.

Filmed a week earlier in front of 13,000 fans at the United Center in Chicago, the two episodes featured such superstars as actors Tom Hanks, Tom Cruise, Katie Holmes (who at the time was married to Tom Cruise), Dakota Fanning, Will Smith, Jada Pinkett Smith, and Halle Berry. Musicians Josh Groban, Patti LaBelle, Beyoncé, Stevie Wonder, Alicia Keys, and Madonna showed up. News anchor Diane Sawyer, child singing sensation Jackie Evancho, and singer, actress, and TV personality Queen Latifah were there, as well as Simon Cowell, Jerry Seinfeld, and Rosie O'Donnell. Even basketball megastar Michael Jordan took to the stage.

What We Know About O

The Oprah Winfrey Show aired 4,561 national episodes in 25 years. Her final episode had the show's highest viewership in 17 years.

Oprah stands on stage at the United Center in Chicago for the first episode, filmed on May 17 and broadcast on May 23, 2011, of the three-episode grand finale of The Oprah Winfrey Show. *Joining her are just a few of the celebrities who showed up to bid a fond farewell to one of the most beloved shows—and hosts—on daytime TV. From left: Oprah, Tom Hanks, Jackie Evancho, Diane Sawyer, Queen Latifah, Patti LaBelle, Beyoncé, Madonna, Dakota Fanning, Halle Berry, Katie Holmes, and Tom Cruise.*

The two gala performances, filmed back-to-back on May 17, were collectively named "Surprise Oprah! A Farewell Spectacular." "Oprah ... didn't know what the shows would entail or who was on the guest list," reported NBC News. "Her producers only told her where and when the shows would be recorded."

Oprah appeared to be genuinely surprised, thrilled, and touched during the four-hour tribute to her and her career.

The last-ever episode of *The Oprah Winfrey Show*, which aired on May 25, 2011, had a completely different tone from this pair of all-star extravaganzas.

During the quiet episode, Oprah thanked her fans and her staff. She spoke about gratitude and success. She played clips from past seasons. In the audience that day were friends and family, including Oprah's longtime beau Stedman Graham, Richard Sher (her co-host from her first talk show), and her fourth-grade teacher and mentor, Mrs. Duncan.

After an hour alone onstage, Oprah looked into the camera and spoke directly to her viewers one last time. "I thank you for being as much of a sweet inspiration for me as I've tried to be for you," she said. "I won't say goodbye. I'll just say 'until we meet again.'"

With that, she stepped off the stage, embraced Stedman, then hugged, kissed, and high-fived crying colleagues. Oprah's little dog Sadie was waiting for her with staff members. Oprah picked up the pooch and told her, "Sadie, we did it!" She then carried the cocker spaniel toward her office as the show ended.

Customers at a bar in Washington, D.C., gather to watch the final episode of The Oprah Winfrey Show *on May 25, 2011.*

O's Best Shows

Over the years, many magazines, websites, and other list-makers have cataloged what they consider Oprah's best-ever shows. Different lists contain different opinions, but some of Oprah's interviews and events are on every list. Here are some of the ones everyone agrees have been her most memorable—from *The Oprah Winfrey Show, Oprah's Next Chapter*, and *Oprah Prime*:

- Oprah reveals her weight loss and pulls a wagon full of fat across the stage, 1988
- Oprah interviews Michael Jackson, 1993
- Ellen DeGeneres "comes out" as a lesbian, 1997
- "You get a car! You get a car!... Everybody gets a car!" 2004
- The Tom Cruise "meltdown," 2005
- Oprah "skewers" author James Frey, 2006
- Whitney Houston admits to "heavy" drug use, 2009
- Rihanna talks about her abuse and how she still loves her abuser, 2009
- Tyler Perry opens up about his childhood of sexual and physical abuse, 2010
- Oprah introduces the half-sister she just discovered, 2011
- Cyclist Lance Armstrong admits he used performing enhancing drugs to win seven Tour de France titles, 2013

Oprah's New World

In January 2011, five months before Oprah took her final bows as host of *The Oprah Winfrey Show*, she launched OWN TV, her specialty cable and satellite channel. In its early months, according to oprah.com, OWN presented "original series and specials, all focused on entertaining, informing and inspiring people to live their best lives."

People from every walk of life found unique ways to honor Oprah during the final year of her show. In this photo, taken a couple of weeks after the last episode of Oprah *aired in 2011, someone in this crowd at the Bonnaroo Music and Arts Festival in Manchester, Tennessee, salutes Oprah with a full-size cardboard cutout that places her right in her element—interacting with an audience! Oprah spent a good part of her childhood in Nashville, which is about 65 miles (105 km) from Manchester.*

"Here was a mammoth TV celebrity who for 25 years did a show that was mostly about telling people to be better to one another and themselves. She may have dabbled in sensationalism and given a platform to hokum like [the self-help book] The Secret, *but she also went into mainstream living rooms to raise awareness about abuse, encourage altruism and foster tolerance. And she did it all with the constant reassurance that her viewers were good people, that they could believe in themselves and that they had the power to make good things happen."*

James Poniewozik, TV critic for *Time* magazine, 2011

Oprah shares a light moment with Tyler Perry at a Hollywood movie premier in 2009. When OWN went through growing pains, Tyler's presence helped get Oprah's network back on track.

The station got off to a rocky start. By the time Oprah's talk show was off the air, OWN was already in trouble. The top executive had already been fired, according to the *Wall Street Journal*, "after months of mediocre ratings and lagging viewership at the channel."

A new CEO took over, but three months later, the network gave him the boot, too, putting Oprah in charge. By then, the cable network was sinking fast. It continued to nose-dive for the next year. In its first 18 months on the air, OWN lost $330 million.

The fast failure of the station was something new to Oprah. "After 25 years of being No. 1, I had become accustomed to success," she said. "I didn't expect failure."

The station's struggle shook her confidence, pushing her to her "breaking point." She said she even experienced symptoms of a nervous breakdown before she turned things around. "I was tested and I had to dig deep" to recover, she said.

The network also managed to recover, largely thanks to actor/producer Tyler Perry. At the end of OWN's second year, Oprah brought him onboard. Since then, Tyler has created a number of successful shows for the network, including *The Haves and the Have*

Nots, Love Thy Neighbor, and *If Loving You Is Wrong*.

OWN is now a success. Oprah's weekly interview show, known as *Oprah's Next Chapter* for the first three years, is now called *Oprah Prime*. It is one of the station's top-rated shows.

Around the time OWN started to get back on track, so did Oprah's film career. In 2013, she co-starred in Lee Daniels' film *The Butler*. She played the wife of the film's title butler. It was her first major movie role since *Beloved* flopped in 1998.

Oprah's performance was called "Oscar-worthy," but she wasn't even nominated for an Academy Award. In fact, the movie didn't score a single Oscar nomination. Another major award competition, the Golden Globes,

Oprah Winfrey and Forest Whitaker in a scene from the 2013 movie The Butler.

also overlooked the film. *The Butler* did win a number of other, lesser known, awards, and Oprah was nominated for Best Supporting Actress in other competitions. But many critics felt Oprah "was robbed."

In 2014, Oprah participated in another high-profile movie project, when she co-produced the civil rights film *Selma*. She also played the small role of activist Annie Lee Cooper in the film.

Selma won an Academy Award for Best Original Song. The film was also nominated for Best Picture, which it didn't win. Critics and viewers were surprised that *Selma* didn't receive more attention at the Oscars.

Oprah may not have been an award-winner, but she still attended the 2015 Academy Awards. She presented the award for Best Adapted Screenplay to screenwriter Graham Moore for *The Imitation Game*, a movie about World War II code breakers.

What We Know About O

In 2013, U.S. President Barack Obama honored Oprah with the highest award he can give to U.S. citizens. He awarded her the Presidential Medal of Freedom because she is "one of the world's most successful broadcast journalists" and philanthropists.

Oprah Winfrey receives the Presidential Medal of Freedom from President Barack Obama on November 20, 2013. Former U.S. president Bill Clinton is shown on the left.

Post-Show O

Now that Oprah no longer hosts a daily talk show, she has time to get involved in other, non-television-related projects.

In the spring of 2014, for example, Oprah moved into the hot beverage business. She partnered with Starbucks Coffee and a tea company called Teavana to create Teavana Oprah Chai Tea. The beverage is sold only at Starbucks. In the words of a Starbucks announcement, "It was personally developed by Oprah Winfrey in close collaboration with Teavana's leading teaologist."

Oprah with Steven Spielberg at the 2014 New York premiere of The Hundred-Foot Journey, *a movie the two produced together.*

This was the first time Oprah had ever put her name on a product or piece of merchandise that was not part of her entertainment empire. Sales of the tea generate donations, which help support youth education and leadership programs. In its first year, sales of Oprah Chai Tea raised more than $5 million for youth programs in the United States and Canada.

Oprah in Miami during her motivational tour, called "The Life You Want," in October 2014.

In the fall of 2014, Oprah launched another new project—a motivational speaking tour. Beginning in September, she took to the road with "The Life You Want Tour." She visited eight cities across the United States, selling out arenas and stadiums everywhere she went.

Early in 2015, Oprah's OWN studios in Los Angeles moved into new headquarters in West Hollywood. Two months later, Oprah announced that Harpo Studios would also move to the new location. This meant that, after 26 years, Oprah would close the Chicago location of Harpo Studios, where she had filmed *The Oprah Winfrey Show*.

"I've spent more hours in this building than I have any other building on Earth," she said after announcing her plans to close Harpo. "The time has come to downsize this part of the business and to move forward. It will be sad to say goodbye, but I look ahead with such a knowing that what the future holds is even more than I can see."

Shortly after announcing the closure of the Chicago studio, Oprah also sold her Chicago apartment. She held an auction sale of the apartment's contents to raise money for her Leadership Academy Foundation. The 500

What We Know About O

The street outside the Harpo Studios building in Chicago was renamed Oprah Winfrey Way in 2011.

items in the sale drew about $800,000 for the cause.

The closure of Harpo Studios in Chicago may have marked the end of a chapter for Oprah, but it allowed her to streamline her life, freeing her up to move in new directions.

"While running OWN will remain a primary focus for [Oprah] going forward, she ... will continue to pursue interests outside of the executive suite," wrote the *Hollywood Reporter* in March 2015. "Recently, [Oprah] announced that she'd be moving in front of the camera at [OWN]... with a recurring role in *Queen Sugar*," a new drama series.

Oprah is also considering performing on Broadway, and she is set to appear in an upcoming movie about actor Richard Pryor. She also plans to pursue international speaking engagements.

The Spinoffs

Some of Oprah's guests over the years were so popular that Oprah—and her Harpo Studios—helped them launch their own television shows.

The first of these was psychologist Dr. Phil McGraw. Oprah met him in 1998, when he helped her prepare for the beef industry trial in Texas. Before long, Dr. Phil, as he came to be known, became a regular guest on Oprah's show. His own show, *Dr. Phil,* took to the airwaves in 2002.

Celebrity chef Rachael Ray launched her cooking show, called *Rachael Ray*, after several appearances on *The Oprah Winfrey Show*.

For five years, beginning in 2004, Dr. Mehmet Oz had a regular segment on *The Oprah Winfrey Show*. He launched his own medical program, *The Dr. Oz Show*, in 2009.

Interior designer Nate Berkus first appeared on Oprah's show in 2002. *The Nate Berkus Show* launched in 2010, but was canceled after two seasons.

Still on Top

Oprah may no longer be beamed into millions of homes every day, but she is still on top of the world. With about $3 billion to her name, she is the richest self-made woman in U.S. history.

In early 2015, her OWN Network logged its highest viewership—and profit—numbers in its four-year history. At the same time, *O, The Oprah Magazine* celebrated its 15th anniversary on newsstands. About 2.4 million people continue to subscribe every month.

Oprah's weekly show, *Oprah Prime*, now in its third season, has been nominated for—and has won—many awards from African-American, gay/lesbian, and other communications organizations.

Oprah is a movie star, film producer, public speaker, talk show host, magazine publisher, and humanitarian. She continues to rank highly on annual lists of the globe's most powerful, richest, and most influential people.

She believes she has a mission in life. "The

Oprah and noted film producer Harvey Weinstein react as TV writer and producer Shonda Rhimes gets up to accept her W. E. B. Du Bois Medal. All three are shown at a 2014 ceremony honoring them and other recipients of Harvard University's award to notable figures in African-American political and cultural achievement.

reason why I'm here is to help connect people to themselves and the higher ideas of consciousness," she said in 2014. "I'm here to help raise consciousness."

No matter what form that mission takes, or what direction Oprah chooses to follow next, she intends to remain true to that mission. She will follow her heart. She will "harness the power of [her] passion." She will do her best to continue to use that super-power for good.

Oprah stops to share some enthusiasm with fans in Denver, Colorado, during her "Live Your Best Life" tour in 2005.

Oprah comforts Mary Lee Quinn, a Hurricane Katrina survivor who is talking about searching for her missing relatives. Oprah found Mary Lee during Oprah's tour of the Astrodome in Houston, Texas, on September 5, 2005. The Astrodome served as a shelter for Katrina survivors who lost their homes in New Orleans, Louisiana, or were forced to evacuate.

Chronology

January 29, 1954 Oprah Gail Winfrey born near Kosciusko, Mississippi; soon after Oprah's birth mother, Vernita, leaves to find work in Milwaukee, Wisconsin; Oprah spends first six years raised by grandparents Hattie Mae and Earless Lee in Mississippi.

1957 Begins reciting verses in front of her church congregation.

1959 Half-sister Patricia born.

1960 Sent to Milwaukee to live with mother; half-brother Jeffrey born.

1962 Sent to Nashville to live with her father Vern and his wife Zelma.

1963 Mother gives birth to another baby girl and gives her up for adoption; Oprah doesn't know about the baby; returns to Milwaukee to live with mother; is raped and later sexually abused for the next five years.

1968 Returns to Nashville to live with father.

1969 Gives birth to a baby boy, who dies a few weeks later.

1970 Invited to give recitation at a church in Los Angeles; while there, decides to become an actress; wins Tennessee state public-speaking competition.

1971 Wins state public-speaking championship for second year; attends White House Conference on Children and Youth in Colorado; wins Miss Fire Prevention title in Nashville; gets job reading news after school on radio station WVOL; graduates from high school and enrolls in Communications and Performing Arts at Tennessee State University.

1972 Named Miss Black Nashville and Miss Black Tennessee; enters Miss Black America but does not win.

1974 Gets job as TV news anchor at WLAC-TV in Nashville.

1975 Quits college, one credit shy of earning diploma.

1976 Becomes news anchor for WJZ-TV in Baltimore, Maryland; meets Gayle King, who becomes Oprah's lifelong best friend.

1977 Removed from anchor desk and moved to less desirable jobs within WJZ-TV newsroom; goes on her first diet.

1978 Becomes co-host of WJZ-TV's new morning talk show, *People are Talking.*

1984 Becomes host of *A.M. Chicago*, a morning talk show in Chicago.

1985 Plays a starring role in the movie *The Color Purple*; *A.M. Chicago* renamed *The Oprah Winfrey Show.*

1986 Creates her production company, Harpo Productions; meets Stedman Graham, who will become her life partner.

1987 Wins her first Daytime Emmy Award for Outstanding Talk Show Host; earns final college credit and graduates from Tennessee State.

1988 Harpo Productions takes ownership of *The Oprah Winfrey Show.*

1989 Half-brother Jeffrey dies of AIDS-related illness.

1996 Launches Oprah's Book Club.

1998 Wins court case after being sued by Texas cattle producers; earns Lifetime Achievement Emmy Award and takes herself out of the running for future Emmys; stars in film called *Beloved*, which is a box office flop; Oprah's Angel Network launched.

1999 Hosts her first annual "Oprah's Favorite Things" episode.

2000 First issue of *O, The Oprah Magazine* hits newsstands.

2003 Half-sister Patricia dies.

2004 Gives every member of her studio audience a car.

2005 Celebrating his love for then-girlfriend (now ex-wife) Katie Holmes, Tom Cruise jumps on Oprah's couch; event causes sensation that Oprah dismisses as media-fueled "brouhaha"; co-produces Broadway version of *The Color Purple*.

2006 Oprah Radio launches.

2007 Opens Oprah Winfrey Leadership Academy for Girls in South Africa; endorses Democratic presidential candidate Barack Obama.

2009 Announces that *The Oprah Winfrey Show* will end in two years.

2010 Discovers she has another half-sister named Patricia, who had been given up for adoption in 1963 and named by adoptive parents.

2011 Introduces newly discovered half-sister on her TV show; two have remained close; launches Oprah Winfrey Network (OWN); May 25, 2011: final episode of *The Oprah Winfrey Show.*

2013 Stars in first film in 15 years, *The Butler*; U.S. president Barack Obama awards Oprah the Presidential Medal of Freedom.

2014 Does eight-city speaking tour called "The Life You Want Tour"; Oprah Radio goes off the air.

2015 Closes Harpo Studios in Chicago.

Glossary

ad lib To speak without a script

affirmative action A system designed to get more women and members of minority groups into jobs, universities, and other organizations

altruism Unselfish concern for others

audition To try out for a role in a play, film, or other performance

boarding house A house where people pay for a room and sometimes daily meals

collectively Together

commencement A graduation ceremony

commentator A person who studies and is an informed speaker about a particular subject

controversial Giving rise to debate or heated disagreement

culture shock The feeling of disorientation or confusion felt by someone who is suddenlty subjected to an unfamiliar culture, lifestyle, or set of attitudes

cynical Believing the worst in people; distrustful of a person's sincerity

demotion Being moved to a lesser job; opposite of a promotion

disadvantaged In an unfavorable situation, especially in regard to social, economic, or educational opportunities

duped Tricked

electrifying Thrilling; exhilarating

empathy The ability to understand and identify with the feelings of others

ethics A set of principles of conduct that govern a person's behavior

exuberance Excitement, enthusiasm

half-brother (or **half-sister**) A child with whom one has only one parent in common

hokum Nonsense

humanitarian A person who works to improve the welfare of others

ill-mannered rude; disrespectful

inner city An area near the center of a city, often associated with economic or social problems

integrate To bring together members of different racial or other groups to achieve equal participation of all members of those groups in a society or institution, such as a school

labor When having to do with pregnancy, the process of childbirth

materialism The tendency to value objects and physical comforts, usually over spiritual values

matron A woman in charge of a group of young people in a school or other institution

mediocre Average; of only moderate quality

motivational Designed to encourage people to take action or become enthusiastic

naive Trusting, childlike, innocent

naysayer Someone who disagrees or opposes

news director The person in charge of a radio or television newsroom

orator A public speaker

perm Short for "permanent wave," a chemical process used to set hair in curls or waves that will last for several months

philanthropist One who donates or raises money for charitable causes

pretentious Making oneself appear smarter or more important, successful, or talented than is true

quota The required number or percentage of something

raped Forced against one's will to have sex, often with the threat or use of violence

revise To change or alter

sensationalism The use of shocking, exaggerated, or dramatic subject matter to get people excited, angry, or otherwise interested

sobriety Being sober; not under the influence of alcohol or drugs

spellbinding Fascinating, holding people's complete attention

streamline To make something run better or more simply

substance abuser Someone who uses alcohol or drugs excessively

syndicated Broadcast by several radio or television stations, usually at the same time, without being carried by a network

tabloid A newspaper or TV show that presents stories that are often not true about scandals, gossip, or other details of celebrities' lives

teleprompter A device attached to a television camera that allows the speaker to read a script while looking into the camera (based on brand name "TelePrompTer")

Tinseltown A nickname for Hollywood

token A member of a minority or underrepresented group who is hired by or admitted to an organization so that the organization has at least one member of that group to give the appearance of equality within the organization

traumatized Experiencing emotional shock or damage

tycoon A wealthy, powerful person in business or industry

Further Information

Books

Cooke, CW. *Female Force: Women in the Media: A Biography Graphic Novel.* Vancouver, WA: Bluewater Productions, 2010.

LaBello, Joshua. *Female Force: Oprah Winfrey: A Graphic Novel.* Vancouver, WA: Bluewater Productions, 2015.

Winfrey, Oprah. *What I Know for Sure*. New York: Flatiron Books, 2014.

Video/DVDs

The Color Purple (VHS/DVD). Amblin Entertainment/Warner Home Video, 1985/2007.

The Oprah Winfrey Show: 20th Anniversary Collection (DVD). Paramount, 2005.

The Women of Brewster Place (DVD). Harpo Productions/Phoenix Entertainment Group, 1989/2011.

Brewster Place (DVD). ABC/Allumination, 1990/2006.

Beloved (VHS/DVD). Touchstone Pictures/Harpo Films, 1998/1999.

Lee Daniels' The Butler (DVD). Weinstein Company/Anchor Bay, 2013/2014.

The Hundred-Foot Journey (DVD). Touchstone Films/Walt Disney Studios Home Entertainment, 2014.

Selma (DVD). Plan B Entertainment/Cloud Eight Films/Harpo Films/Pathé, 2014/2015.

Websites

youtube.com/watch?v=xLRktpZ1C8o
"Oprah Reflects on Tom Cruise's Couch Jumping." Although Oprah won't show Tom Cruise's athletics on any of her authorized websites, they can be found elsewhere on YouTube. In this clip, Oprah talks about the day Tom jumped on and off—and on and off—her couch.

youtube.com/watch?v=WmCQ-V7c7Bc
"Oprah Relives the Famous Car Giveaway." Oprah talks about the famous car giveaway episode and replays the most exciting part of the episode.

youtube.com/playlist?list=PLCBC8C65C2C23F793
"*TV Guide Magazine*'s Top 25 Best 'Oprah Show' Moments." *TV Guide* and the Oprah Winfrey Network (OWN) have compiled a video collection of what they consider to be *The Oprah Winfrey Show*'s most memorable moments.

biography.com/people/oprah-winfrey-9534419
"Oprah Winfrey Biography." On this site, you can watch a short video about Oprah's life, along with a written biography.

achievement.org/autodoc/page/win0int-1
"America's Best Friend." In 1989, Oprah was inducted into the Academy of Achievement, an organization designed to introduce students to inspirational people. In February 1991, the Academy interviewed Oprah. Here, the interview is presented as a written document, but also includes video clips of the interview.

youtube.com/watch?v=eNmVhSClh8g
"Watch the 25-Year Evolution of Oprah's Hairstyle in Less Than 2 Minutes." In this video clip, produced by OWN TV in 2015, Oprah provides a quick review of some of the many do's (and a few don't's!) she has sported over the decades.

youtube.com/watch?v=YzYPJV9LtJg
"The Ultimate Viewers Win a Trip to Australia." During the first episode of the 25th and final season of *The Oprah Winfrey Show*, Oprah surprised the show's entire audience of "Ultimate Viewers," which reportedly drew its members from the United States, Canada, and Jamaica, with a trip to Australia. In this clip, Oprah reveals how she planned her surprise and tricked her audience into believing that they were being snubbed in favor of an earlier studio audience.

Index

About the Author

Diane Dakers was born and raised in Toronto and now makes her home in Victoria, British Columbia. Diane has been a newspaper, magazine, television, and radio journalist since 1991. Like Oprah, she loves interviewing fascinating people. Unlike Oprah, she is not a billionaire.